Working with Parents, Carers and Families in the Early Years

Parents have a crucial role in supporting children's learning, development and well-being. The act of forming effective partnerships with families and carers is a key feature of the Early Years Foundation Stage. Achieving this takes time, reflective practice, skill and a solid understanding of the barriers that can impede forming effective working relationships with parents.

This guide offers an informed and comprehensive framework for working with parents, drawing on the latest evidence and containing practical advice from practitioners and parents, to support sound partnership practice. Full of examples and activities for training and resources to support practice across a wide range of settings, it focuses on key areas such as:

- working with parents of different aged children
- the development of strategies to support the relationship
- the barriers to partnership working, including cultural differences and working with hard-to-reach families
- setting up home and setting visits
- creating parent-friendly environments.

Including case studies, questions for reflective practice and chapter links to Early Years Teachers' Standards, this book will be ideal for early years students on Foundation Degrees, Childhood Studies courses and those training to become early years teachers, as well as early years practitioners and managers responsible for staff training.

Teresa Wilson is Programme Director for the Foundation Degree in Children's Development and Learning at the University of Reading, UK.

Working with Parents, Carers and Families in the Early Years

The essential guide

Teresa Wilson

Routledge
Taylor & Francis Group

LONDON AND NEW YORK

First published 2016
by Routledge
2 Park Square, Milton Park, Abingdon, Oxon OX14 4RN

and by Routledge
711 Third Avenue, New York, NY 10017

Routledge is an imprint of the Taylor & Francis Group, an informa business

British Library Cataloguing in Publication Data
A catalogue record for this book is available from the British Library

Library of Congress Cataloging-in-Publication Data
Wilson, Teresa.
Working with parents, carers and families in the early years : the essential
guide / Teresa Wilson.
   pages cm
   Includes bibliographical references.
   1. Early childhood education–Parent participation. 2. Parent-teacher
relationships. 3. Home and school. 4. Communication in education. I. Title.
   LB1139.35.P37W56 2015
   372.21–dc23   2015007061

ISBN: 978-0-415-72871-3 (hbk)
ISBN: 978-0-415-72874-4 (pbk)
ISBN: 978-1-315-69120-6 (ebk)

Typeset in Bembo
by Wearset Ltd, Boldon, Tyne and Wear

Printed in Great Britain by Ashford Colour Press Ltd

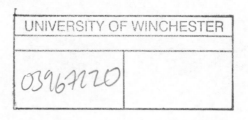

Thank you:

To colleagues, practitioners and parents who have participated in the research undertaken for this book.

To all of my family for their support and love, and especially to my husband, Rick, for all those jobs that you did to save me thinking about them.

To the editorial teams at Taylor & Francis and Wearset for their patience and support, especially Sarah Richardson and Hannah Riley.

Contents

Illustrations

Figures

Tables

Acknowledgements

Thanks to all practitioners, members of teaching staff and parents from these schools, colleges and early years settings who took the time and trouble to contribute or signpost to the survey that has in part informed my book. I received contributions from:

Berkshire
Buckinghamshire
Cambridgeshire
Cornwall
Devon
East Sussex
Hertfordshire
Lancashire
London
Middlesex

Thanks go to these settings for distributing surveys:

Alconbury Pre-School
Ascot and Cranbourne Pre-School
Bassingbourn Primary School
Chesterton Children's Centre
Children's Centres in Preston
City College, Plymouth
Kingston College – Foundation Degree in Leadership and Management in Early Years
Little Angels Pre-School in Plymouth
Rectory Lane Pre-School, Bracknell
St Winifred's RC Primary School, London SE12
And various childminder settings

Thanks also to the following people for their help by giving permission to use parts of their work, or for talking to me and guiding my thoughts:

Katy Downs
Jo Elsey
David Howe
Lorraine Khan
Juliet Neill-Hall

Their contribution has helped me enormously in the shaping of the book but any errors or omissions are mine alone.

Introduction

Research suggests that not all parents feel confident in engaging with early years settings or schools (Devine, 2004; Ball, 2003) and that there can often also be a mismatch around the expectations of involvement between parents and staff. Yet there is also extensive evidence which demonstrates the importance of the role of the parent and family in children's development. Desforges and Abouchaar (2003), for example, concluded that parental involvement 'has a major effect on school outcomes even after all other forces (e.g. the effect of poor attainment or of social class) have been factored out' (p. 10). Furthermore, researchers in the past decade have shown that parental involvement is also influential in pre-school settings (Melhuish et al., 2008; Evangelou et al., 2007) and can have an impact on children's social and emotional development (Wheeler et al., 2009), language and literacy development and development of mathematical language (Evangelou et al., 2009). It can be assumed, therefore, that a constructive relationship between a setting and parents or carers is a factor that may improve outcomes for children.

In the early years sector, there is widespread engagement with the notion of partnership with parents; however, the term 'partnership' can be misleading as definitions are inconsistent (MacGiolla, 2005), leading to a wide variety in the development of relationships between settings and families. This book, therefore, stems from an interest in the relationship between practitioners and parents and draws on my own experience of working with parents and practitioners for over 20 years, which has observed that partnership with parents is implemented in a wide variety of ways, meaning different things to different people.

In the year 2012–13, over four million families (with over six million children) were using some form of childcare arrangements for children between birth and 14 years. That is 78 per cent of all families with children of this age (Department for Education (DfE), 2014a, p. 12). Whilst school-aged children will attend institutions which have a certain uniformity about them as they will need to conform to either the National Curriculum, Ofsted or the Independent Schools Inspectorate, the pre-school years are populated with a range of provision and England's history of fragmented early years care and education is reflected in the range of services available to parents and their children.

> Before Labour's new government, pre-school education in England, and in the UK generally, was patchy, with some services provided by the Local Education Authority or Social Services departments, some run by voluntary bodies such as the Pre-school Learning Alliance, and others provided by the private sector.
>
> (Sylva et al., 2010, p. 2)

Historically, private, voluntary and independent settings have operated within the UK, all of which must now be registered with the government inspectorate body (Ofsted) in order to deliver the Early Years Foundation Stage (EYFS). In addition to these, there is a national network of Sure Start Children's Centres whose purpose, 'revised in 2012, is to improve child development, school readiness, parenting aspirations and skills, and child and family health and life chances with a particular focus on the most disadvantaged families' (DfE, 2014a, p. 28). Although settings are standardised in that they are governed by the same statutory framework (DfE, 2014b), and deliver the EYFS, and use the same qualified staff, their historical contexts and values vary significantly and the services that they deliver also have distinctive features. It follows, then, that the parents who choose to use the settings may also have differing philosophies or needs.

So, Children's Centres offer a range of additional services for parents (now more targeted than universal), pre-schools tend to be sessional and part-time, daycare offers full-time provision, and wraparound services support provision for parents who are unable to collect children themselves. Further options are available from settings which follow particular pedagogical principles, including Montessori and Steiner provision.

From this rich diversity of definitions within a wide range of provision, the decision to carry out research into partnership with parents was taken during 2014. The specific research questions I was interested in were:

Q. What do practitioners and parents understand partnership to be?

Q. What factors enhance partnership and what detracts from it?

By considering the perspectives of both parents and early years practitioners, the expectations – as well as similarities and differences in these – could be explored. Such an understanding is important if we are to promote positive engagement and relationships.

People who might find this book useful

People who might find this book useful include: early years professionals, early years teachers and other early years practitioners; parenting practitioners and family support workers; workers in Children's Centres; and practitioners and students working towards a Foundation Degree or a BA in Early Childhood Studies, Child Development, or a range of related programmes, in particular those aimed at practitioners.

The parenting workforce

There is a wide range of practitioners who are working with parents. Some are based in the parenting sector, so they not only work with parents but they are actively involved in supporting parents in their role of being a parent. Some will have a less direct role in working with parents. The midwife or a parenting practitioner will have an intensive relationship, primarily with parents, whilst many occupations will have more peripheral roles which involve supporting children and families in a range of ways. The Common Core of Skills and Knowledge (Children's Workforce Development Council (CWDC), 2010) was developed during the Labour administration (1997 and 2010), when significant investment was made into family support through the development of, amongst other things, Sure Start Children's Centres. The Common Core guidance focuses on a number of areas and 'describes the skills and knowledge that everyone who works with children and young people is expected to have ... reflecting a set of common values for practitioners that promote equality, respect diversity and challenge stereotypes' (CWDC, 2010, p. 2).

Summary of the book's contents, chapter by chapter

Chapter 1

This chapter sets the scene for the exploration of some of the main elements of partnership with parents. The first section focuses on the changes that have taken place within the family and within society in the UK and also globally in terms of population and migration patterns, and family and relationship patterns. These patterns result in a more diverse community of parents in settings. The chapter also looks at some of the main theories in relation to child development and also to families, including (but not limited to) Bronfenbrenner's ecological systems theory (2005), Bandura's social learning theory (1977), attachment theory with a range of theorists (Bowlby, 1953; Elfer *et al.*, 2003; Howe, 2011; Rutter, 1987), Baumrind's parenting styles (1991) and the role of the adult to support learning (Vygotsky, 1978).

This chapter examines the core function of the book: the rationale behind working with parents in terms of building trusting relationships in order to improve outcomes for children.

Chapter 2

This chapter positions the principles and background to parent-partnership practice within the policy, legislative and theoretical frameworks. It will start from the landscape within which we are now working, and look back on recent policy and legislation, as well as exploring the recent change of priority in terms of working with parents. We shall explore the National Occupational Standards for Work with Parents (Lifelong Learning UK, 2011) and Common Core of Skills and Knowledge for working with parents (CWDC). A number of policies have been developed by different governments and they form the structure of expectations for working with parents within registered settings. This section will expand on the development of the frameworks and observe how they interact.

Then we shall look at relevant legislation and how it fits in with the current Children's Workforce. In addition to the policy frameworks, we will explore the many recurring themes within the legislative framework, especially in those statutes enacted over the past 25 years. This section will note where the practitioners' responsibilities lie in terms of legal obligations. It will also look at the development of professional qualifications by successive governments and inform about the current position.

Chapter 3

In order to work effectively with parents, it is important to understand our own perceptions of parenting and parenthood. This is an important chapter because it recognises the way that we all categorise experiences. Our own experiences of being parented can have an influence on our practice and on our values. This chapter explores the relationship between the professional and the personal and how those two areas can be reconciled when working in the Children's Workforce. A range of theorists whose work involves reflective practice will be introduced or re-introduced: Dewey, Schön, Moon and Lindon.

Chapter 4

This chapter looks at the importance of transition preparation, including home and setting visits and how to prepare for them. There is some discussion about the desirability of home visits, and whether it is an intrusion or an important opportunity to learn how to support the child. Much of its value will depend on the skills of the practitioners making the visits. This chapter will explore the debates and the strategies that can be used to make the visit effective and also safe for both the practitioner and the family.

It is not always possible to carry out home visits so this section will also look at the ways that the initial setting visits can be as effective and fruitful as possible, with consideration of expectations, preparation and information-sharing opportunities. It will also link to the value of working effectively with professionals from other settings.

Chapter 5

Each section within this chapter looks at the needs of children and families at particular ages and stages. The focus is on infants, toddlers, pre-schoolers and children with disabilities, looking at particular issues relating to children within each age and/or stage, and how to work effectively with parents during these phases.

So, the parents of a first baby will have different needs to those of a pre-schooler whose child is preparing to start school. When considering transition processes, strategies to involve parents, such as to gain information from parents to pass on, and to ensure parental involvement in the process, will be considered.

Chapter 6

This chapter will identify how to make a setting appealing to families. It will make an assessment of what works for parents, and consider how settings can be inclusive to all family members (including fathers, grandparents and those whose first language is not English).

It will also include a discussion about the reality of partnership work and how settings adjust the way practitioners and parents engage together so that the environment is based on partnership, giving children opportunities to share their home lives and practitioners opportunities to develop their planning based, in some part, on the home experiences of the child.

Chapter 7

There are opportunities to extend children's learning when links are made between the home and the setting. This section identifies how to build on those links and how to engage parents in a dialogue relating to their child's development that can extend ideas and promote development.

Different types of communication are explored, with reference to Epstein's typology of family involvement (Epstein, 1995), learning journals and the philosophies of Te Whāriki and Reggio Emilia.

Chapter 8

There are a number of barriers to partnership work: hard-to-reach families who fear authority; families who perceive themselves to be different; busy families; sick parents; parents who believe it is not their role to engage with the setting. This section considers (through the voices of practitioners and parents) the ways that we may unconsciously prevent families from engaging with a setting, and considers ways to break down barriers.

Chapter 9

This final chapter hopes to draw together the themes from the book:

- the prevailing views from my research
- key theories
- improving outcomes through relationship building.

Questions are raised about the opportunities that present themselves and whether practitioners make the most of the opportunities that they have and what else we can do to build part of the community which should surround all children, giving support and information to parents and care and education to children.

Summary

This book, therefore, is a combination of literature from this field and other relevant areas, voices of practitioners and parents, opportunities for reflection and a selection of activities to encourage change and innovation within settings. There is never time or space to write everything, but I hope that this is a good start on the journey to true partnership with parents.

I hope that this book will raise understanding of prevailing attitudes and perceptions in relation to the parent/setting partnership and will enable practitioners to reflect upon practice that can support the relationship and, therefore, raise opportunities to improve outcomes for children.

References

Ball, S.J. (2003) *Class Strategies and the Education Market: The Middle Classes and Social Advantage.* London: Routledge Falmer.

Bandura, A. (1977) *Social Learning Theory.* Englewood Cliffs, NY: Prentice Hall.

Baumrind, D. (1991) The influence of parenting style on adolescence competence and substance use. *Journal of Early Adolescence,* 11: 56–95.

Bowlby, J. (1953) *Childcare and the Growth of Love.* London: Penguin.

Bronfenbrenner, U. (2005) *Making Human Beings Human: Bioecological Perspectives on Human Development.* London: Sage Publications.

Children's Workforce Development Council (CWDC) (2010) *The Common Core of Skills and Knowledge for the Children and Young People's Workforce*. Leeds: CWDC. Online: http://webarchive.nationalarchives.gov.uk/20120119192332/http://cwdcouncil.org.uk/assets/0000/9297/CWDC_CommonCore7.pdf (accessed 17 August 2014).

Department for Education (DfE) (2014a) *Childcare and Early Years Survey of Parents*. London: DfE.

Department for Education (DfE) (2014b) *Early Years Foundation Stage: Statutory Framework*. London: DfE.

Desforges, C. and Abouchaar, A. (2003) *The Impact of Parental Involvement, Parental Support and Family Education on Pupil Achievements and Adjustment: A Literature Review*, RR433. London: DfES.

Devine, F. (2004) *Class Practices: How Parents Help Their Children Get Good Jobs*. Cambridge: Cambridge University Press.

Elfer, P., Goldschmeid, E. and Selleck, D. (2003) *Key Persons in the Nursery: Building Relationships for Quality Provision*. London: David Fulton.

Epstein, J. (1995) School/family/community partnerships: caring for the children we share. *The Phi Delta Kappa*, 76(9): 701–712.

Evangelou, M., Brooks, G. and Smith, S. (2007) The Birth to School Study: evidence on the effectiveness of PEEP, an early intervention for children at risk of educational underachievement. *Oxford Review of Education*, 33(5): 581–609.

Evangelou, M., Sylva, K. and Kyriacou, M. (2009) *Early Years Learning and Development: Literature Review*. London: DCSF.

Howe, D. (2011) *Attachments Across the Lifecourse: A Brief Introduction*. Basingstoke: Palgrave Macmillan.

Lifelong Learning UK (2011) *National Occupational Standards for Work with Parents*. Online: http://pelorous.totallyplc.com/media_manager/public/115/publications/Qualifications/work-with-parents-nos-jan-2011.pdf (accessed 17 August 2014).

MacGiolla, P.B. (2005) The challenges of partnership: an examination of parent–teacher meetings and school reports in the context of partnership. *Irish Educational Studies*, 24(1): 93–104.

Melhuish, E.C., Mai, B. Phan, M.P., Sylva, K., Sammons, P., Siraj-Blatchford, I. and Taggart, B. (2008) Effects of the home learning environment and preschool centre experience upon literacy and numeracy development in early primary school. *Journal of Social Issues*, 64(1): 95–114.

Rutter, M. (1987) Psychosocial resilience and protective mechanisms. *American Journal of Orthopsychiatry*, 57(3): 316–330.

Sylva, K., Melhuish, E., Sammons, P., Siraj-Blatchford, I. and Taggart, B. (eds) (2010) *Early Childhood Matters: Evidence from the Effective Pre-School and Primary Education Project*. Abingdon: Routledge

Vygotsky, L. (1978) *Mind in Society*. Cambridge, MA: Harvard University Press.

Wheeler, H., Connor, J. and Goodwin, H. (2009) *Parents, Early Years and Learning: Parents as Partners in the Early Years Foundation Stage: Principles Into Practice*. London: NCB.

Chapter 1

Introducing families, theory and partnership work

The importance of working in partnership with parents

In this chapter, we shall be looking at:

- parental involvement in education
- the diverse nature of the family
- theories relating to the family
- risk and resilience
- parenting styles
- what partnership is, and why it is important.

The importance of developing positive relationships and strong engagements with parents in order to enhance the learning and development of children has not always been recognised: indeed, it was not until the 1944 Education Act that there was any specific mention of parental input as a principle in key legislation and even from that point and onwards to the Plowden Report in 1967, there was an implicit view that parents were seen as 'a problem rather than a support for schools' (Muschamp *et al.*, 2007, p. 4) and the purpose of schools was partly to make up for the shortfalls of some parents. This assumption has been overturned through a proliferation of evidence, which has established that children benefit from the involvement of parents in their learning (Desforges and Abouchaar, 2003; Melhuish *et al.*, 2008; Sylva *et al.*, 2004). For example, there is now clear evidence that:

- 'Parents' influence is important throughout childhood and adolescence' Department for Education and Skills (DfES, 2007, p. 5).
- 'Recent research has shown the importance of parental warmth, stability, consistency and boundary setting in helping children develop ... skills' (DfES, 2007, p. 5).
- 'There is clearly significant public interest in making it as easy as possible for parents – fathers and mothers – to engage as partners in their children's learning and development from the earliest age' (DfES, 2007, p. 6).
- 'The home learning environment is important for school readiness in addition to benefits associated with pre-school' (Melhuish *et al.*, 2008, p. 108).
- 'The most important finding from the point of view of this review is that parental involvement in the form of "at home good parenting" has a significant positive effect on children's achievement and adjustment even after all other factors shaping attainment have been taken out of the equation.... The scale of the impact is evident across all social classes and all ethnic groups' (Desforges and Abouchaar, 2003, p. 4).
- 'Many professionals in contact with families have brief and important opportunities to identify and mobilise support for children with persistent behavioural problems' (Khan, 2014, p. 13).

To sum up, a positive and healthy relationship between parent and child supports development and learning. It is in the interests of everyone (children, families, practitioners, wider society) to support 'at home good parenting' (Desforges and Abouchaar, 2003, p. 4).

Parents and education: a brief history

Parents were not always seen as their child's 'first and most enduring educator', as they are today (Qualifications and Curriculum Authority/Department for Education and Employment, 2000, p. 9). Neither have they universally been considered a positive influence on their children – for example, when raising their children in poverty during the Industrial Revolution at the beginning of the nineteenth century. During that time, there was widespread enforced emigration of children to the colonies: New Zealand, Canada, South Africa and Australia, largely because: 'Emigration enthusiasts generally believed that poverty and crime were the result of a lack of moral rectitude' and therefore the removal of children of the poor 'sought to prevent the children from sabotaging the nation' (Bates, 2009, p. 146). The approach between then and now has changed considerably.

It was not until the Industrial Revolution that there was a growing and widespread need for parents to find childcare for their children. Prior to this, children would accompany their parents in their work within rural communities, or be cared for by extended family members (Burnette, 2008). However, the 'movement of work into factories increased the difficulty of combining work and childcare. In most factory work the hours were rigidly set, and women who took the jobs had to accept the twelve or thirteen hour days' (Burnette, 2008, p. 15). As women's economic role has increased and families have dispersed geographically, so has the need for childcare increased beyond the family. It can be seen through statistical data that women with children are represented to much the same extent in terms of numbers as those without children:

> The gap in employment rates for women with and without children has narrowed over the last fifteen years, from 5.8 percentage points in 1996 to just 0.8 percentage points in the final quarter of 2010. In this quarter, 66.5 per cent of mothers were in work and 67.3 per cent of women without a dependent child were in work.
>
> (Office for National Statistics, 2011, p. 2)

The diverse nature of the family

A contemporary model of the family could be more challenging to define than more traditional models. The word 'family' can have a wider meaning for some than others; it can refer to closest friends as well as family (Mason and Tipper, 2008). The saying: 'it takes a village to raise a child' also implies that 'family' can mean those who live and perhaps work together in a community.

A family today could be one of a range of models. It is unlikely to comply with anthropologist George Murdock's 1949 definition of the family: 'Characterised by common residence, economic cooperation and reproduction. It includes adults of both sexes, at least two of whom maintain a socially approved sexual relationship, and one or more children, own or adopted, of the sexually cohabiting adults' (cited in Yeo and Lovell, 2003). This model does not take into account that 'children are now likely to experience a variety of family structures before adulthood' (Panico et al., 2010, p. 3).

> **Activity**
>
> What characteristics do you recognise in the definition above? Do most of the people you know fit into the definition and, if they don't, how could you adapt it so it was more inclusive of all families?

If we understand the purpose of the family to be sexual, economic, reproductive and educational, a micro-group of society which economically supports members of the family group and socialises children to live within the norms of a particular society, then all of the above models are compliant. Additional complexities are added when social norms, values or expectations within sub-cultures of social groups are contrasting, leading to some need for transition management when children move from one dominant cultural expectation to another, as a child might move from their home to an early education or care setting.

Our own childhoods and the expectations, values and habits from our own family life will have given us our assumed model of what a family is, but there are many different styles of family. Our experiences are unique and will shape values and behaviours. The range of family frameworks extends from the nuclear family of parents and children to the extended family of three or more generations living close to each other; from same-sex parents to the kinship of close friends who have become 'like parents' (Mason and Tipper, 2008); from protected children to neglected children.

All the family members can have an influence on the dynamic and behaviour of the family as a whole (see family systems theory and ecological systems theory in Chapter 2). So when the family surrounding the child is considered, there may be many more family members who have an influence. As a practitioner, you may want to reflect upon whether your relationship is solely with the primary carer who brings and collects the child from your setting, or with other members of the family, including fathers and grandparents, as well as siblings.

> In general, fathers are still less visible than mothers within the education system. In a survey: 'When asked who was most involved in their child's school life – them or their partner, mothers were almost five times more likely than fathers to say they were most involved' (DfE, 2010, p. 2).

Theories relating to the family

Attachment theory

Attachment theory demonstrates the function of the relationship between caregiver and infant/child in terms of security, safety and predictable behaviour. A child who is securely attached (who has a close and warm bond) to their primary carer (or carers) has a base from which it is possible to explore, discover and take risks, in which to learn and grow, in the knowledge that the carer consistently offers a place of safety. John Bowlby was the originator of attachment theory (Bowlby, 1953). His hypothesis was that children need a primary carer (usually the mother) to form a relationship with, which produces a secure attachment, and without the relationship, the 'separation and loss' felt by the child has an impact on future learning and social and emotional development.

From the point of view of the child, the purpose of attachment behaviour is to maintain a warm and sensitive relationship with their caregiver. Therefore, the varieties of attachment behaviour will elicit distinct responses, depending on their relationship with their caregiver (who, in terms of the child, is their source of life, food, safety). If the caregiver declines to engage in a securely attached relationship (often as a result of not experiencing it in their own childhood) the child still needs to maintain contact, in order, biologically, to stay alive. Therefore they will adapt their attachment behaviour in order to 'attain and/or maintain a desired proximity' (Bowlby, 1997, p. 371), which is dictated by the caregiver.

Attachment is closely linked to the concept of the internal working model and the development of self-concept. A child that has a secure attachment to a primary carer is said to have a secure base from which to explore and to return in the knowledge of their constancy and availability. This in turn generates a positive sense of self for the child which will inform their internal working model of their value in terms of their relationships with others: 'Repeated experiences of interacting with attachment figures allow infants gradually to develop mental representations (internal working models) of their own worthiness based on other people's availability and their ability and willingness to provide care and protection' (Howe, 2011, p. 33).

Mary Ainsworth and colleagues (Ainsworth *et al.*, 1978) conducted research into different patterns of behaviour patterns and identified three patterns of attachment: secure, insecure/avoidant and ambivalent.

In his book, *Attachment Across the Lifecourse* (Howe, 2011), Howe depicts the ensuing impact of attachment relationships and the possible related outcomes. See Table 1.1.

Asmussen (2011, p. 76) notes that 'Attachment research highlights the idea that a warm and sensitive caregiving environment is central to adaptive and competent child development' and, whilst this may indicate that the absence of a secure attachment with a primary carer may have negative effects on a child's optimum development, it is also possible that the presence of a key person may alleviate some of the worst effects. However, there should be a significant number of 'checks and balances' (Elfer *et al.*, 2003, p. 55) to ensure that the warm relationship that may evolve between a key person and a child maintains professional boundaries. This is something that can be supported through the effective use of supervision, a statutory requirement of the Early Years Foundation Stage (3.21) (DfE, 2014).

Social learning theory

Albert Bandura's theory of social learning (1977) was based on the proposition that children learn through watching and imitating. In his notable experiment, the impact of motivation and reinforcement of behaviour was shown through the observation of children's reactions to a film of an adult repeatedly hitting a large doll (Bobo). The experiment indicated that modelling can have both positive and negative outcomes, depending on who is being observed and their relationship to the child, but a number of criteria also influence the outcome. These include:

*   attention – this might include the frequency of seeing the action
*   retention – the behaviour is more likely to be retained if the information is considered important
*   reproduction – it must be possible to reproduce the behaviour
*   motivation – there must be a reason for repeating the behaviour.

(cited in Asmussen, 2011, p. 121)

Table 1.1 Attachment model

| *Organised* | | |
Insecure–Avoidant (A)	Secure (B) 55–60%	Insecure–Ambivalent (C)
Self: Unloved but self-reliant.	Self: Loved, effective, autonomous and competent.	Self: Low value, ineffective and dependent.
Other people: Rejecting and intrusive.	Other people: Available, cooperative and dependable.	Other people: Insensitive, inconsistent, unpredictable and unreliable.
Parent rebuffs. Distress fails to increase responsiveness. Children are tolerated if undemanding. Children learn to contain feelings and don't indicate vulnerability.	Unconditional, sense of trust.	Exaggerated display of needs to get attention of unresponsive carer. Whiney, clingy. Fighting for attention.
Internal working model = unloved and unlovable. Consistently unresponsive.	Internal working model = lovable and loved. Consistency and responsiveness.	Internal working model = low sense of worth, ineffective and dependant.
Expressions of need and distress are kept low, contained or hidden. Play and exploration maintained at the expense of attachment.	Needs expressed – distress soothed appropriately in contact with caregiver. Infants play with confidence when attachment system not active.	Expressions of need exaggerated and prolonged. Infants not readily soothed by their carers.

A, B and C are all called 'organised' attachments: 'Despite their anxiety, ambivalent and avoidant infants have been able to adapt to their parents and select, evaluate and modify their behaviour in a manner that allows them to achieve proximity and contact when needed.'

Disorganised (D)
Self: Unloved, alone and frightened.
Other people: Frightening, rejecting and unavailable.
Attachment figure is often the cause of distress – e.g. abusive or emotionally unavailable (substance abuse, depression), failing to protect (neglectful), frightening children and failing to resolve child's fearful state. Whatever strategy the children uses, it fails to bring proximity or comfort.
Internal working model = frightened, alone, dangerous, bad.

Note
An adaptation of David Howe (2011) *Attachment Across the Lifecourse*. Basingstoke: Palgrave Macmillan – pages 44–49.

In the case of the Bobo doll shown in Bandura's experiment, the changes of behaviour when children observed different adults behaving aggressively to a large doll were triggered not only by the behaviour they observed but also by the sanctions delivered to those carrying out the behaviour. This is an extension of Skinner's behaviourist theory of reinforcement, because what Bandura claimed was that children 'will increase certain behaviours if they see others being rewarded for the same actions' (Asmussen, 2011, p. 80).

In terms of relevance to parenting, the proximity and repetitive nature of behaviours which take place in the family home may indicate that, if behaviour is reinforced by approval from others, it is more likely to be imitated. So social learning through modelling desired behaviour can be a powerful strategy for parents, or indeed practitioners, to use either consciously or unconsciously. It is likely to have a more substantial impact if the behaviour is carried out by someone who is admired by the observer, so a close relationship between a parent and child is more likely to reinforce the behaviour. If there is not a warm and loving relationship, the child is less motivated to behave in this way. The ways in which children learn through social interactions also resonates with Vygotsky's theory (1978) of children's learning 'through their social environment and specifically with adult guidance operating within a child's "zone of proximal development"', (Melhuish et al., 2008, p. 108) and again can lead to opportunities for parents and practitioners to support children's development through a shared understanding of a child's interests and abilities.

Bronfenbrenner's human ecological model

For Uri Bronfenbrenner, the family is but one part of the environment which influences child development: it is 'the filter through which the larger society influences child development' (Bee and Boyd, 2010, p. 338).

Bronfenbrenner's ecological systems theory (Bronfenbrenner, 2005) asserts that there are many influences on development, and these interact within and beyond certain strata within society. So, in the centre is the child and the immediate family (the microsystem), where the most direct areas of contact and influence lie. The child might be affected by the number of siblings in the family, or the extent of the resources in the home. This could include wider members of the family, nursery settings and schools. But beyond that is another layer of wider influence that is stratified within the exosystem, which are elements that affect the child even though the child does not have a direct relationship with that element. This could include the employment of the parent, so the child would be affected both economically and emotionally if a parent was made redundant. Finally, the earlier systems rest within the community mesosystem and cultural macrosystem of that society, so elements such as the political and economic system or the prevailing religious culture would also have an impact on the child.

Family systems theory

It may be clearer to look at the role of families in society through the 'family systems theory', which suggests that families are one part of the anthropological structure of society which function within a social system and have various practices which support the existence and development of society. So, a family member will have a number of roles both within their family and also in the ways that they relate to the outside world. Each family is likely to organise their family systems in their own way, though there will be cultural similarities within groups. Additional cultural differences may affect the way that the family members are able to integrate within other parts of society, and this, plus their socio-economic status, can have an impact on access to services, education and acceptance. Indeed, Fuller comments, in relation to Pierre Bourdieu's theory on power through capital, that the 'greater an individual's social, cultural and economic capital, the greater their ability to ... achieve educational success' (Fuller, 2014, p. 131).

There are a number of other theories that are closely linked to the structure and functions of the family, and that also relate closely to family systems theory in that the social unit is seen as having an impact on the behaviour of all participants in that unit, including attachment theory, ecological systems theory and social learning theory.

Social anthropology gives us more information on the role and purpose of the family, though again each generation develops its own interpretation of the value and purpose of social systems including the family. We shall see in the next chapter the ways that society implements change through legislation.

Reducing risk and increasing resilience in children

In order to develop – intellectually, emotionally, socially and morally – a child requires, for all of these, the same thing: participation in progressively more complex activities, on a regular basis over an extended period of time in the child's life, with one or more persons with whom the child develops a strong, mutual, emotional attachment, and who are committed to the child's well-being and development, preferably for life.

(Bronfenbrenner, 2005, p. 9)

Bronfenbrenner aptly sums up one of the protective factors which impact on children's development: warm attachment relationships. This is only one of a number of factors that have been identified as being protective to children's well-being, outcomes and mental health as they grow up (Blanden, 2006; Stewart *et al.*, 1997; Rutter, 1987). Other factors include good health, easy temperament and adequate housing – they can all be seen in Table 1.2.

Activity

Use Table 1.2 to reflect on your practice. You will see that there are blank columns and that the table is divided into three domains: Individual (child), Family and Social/ environmental.

Think about the protective factors in the context of those domains, so, for example, you can see that positive self-esteem is a protective factor for the child. Consider how you raise children's self-esteem (perhaps through positive praise strategies, display of child's drawings, etc.) and put that in the second column. Then reflect on other strategies you could develop, such as leading a training session in your setting, to raise awareness of the importance of self-esteem. Include that in the third column. Then do the same with the other protective factors. Some strategies will cross from one domain to another. You can complete this alone or as a study/CPD activity.

Parenting styles

The parent–child relationship is thought to be highly significant in terms of the acquisition of developmental outcomes for children (Desforges and Abouchaar, 2003). A strong and affectionate relationship can 'buffer the child against the negative effects of otherwise disadvantageous environments' (Bee and Boyd, 2010, p. 342). A warm and supportive parent is viewed as an important resource associated with positive developmental outcomes, which correlates to the research by Maccoby and Martin (1983) and also by Baumrind (1991), which identified four parenting styles – authoritarian, authoritative, neglectful, permissive (see Figure 1.1).

Table 1.2 Protective factors (from Blanden, 2006; Rutter, 1987; Stewart et al., 1997)

How can we increase protective factors for children?

Domain or ecological level	What are you doing already?	What else can you do?	Protective factors
Individual (child)			Good health and development Above-average intelligence Hobbies and interests Good peer relationships *Personality factors:* Easy temperament Positive disposition Active coping style Positive self-esteem Good social skills Internal locus of control Success in non-academic pursuits
Family			Secure attachment Warm parent–child relationship Supportive family environment Household rules Parental monitoring Parental interest in education Extended family support and involvement, including childcare Stable relationship with child Good parental coping skills Family expectations of pro-social behaviour and a positive future High parental education
Social/environmental			Mid-to-high socio-economic status Access to health care and social services Adequate housing Family religious faith participation Positive school experiences Supportive adults outside of family Hobbies and pastimes

The styles vary in terms of control and warmth to children. Thus, the neglectful parent is low in both control and nurturing, paying little attention to the child whether their behaviour is prosocial or anti-social. The permissive parent is high in nurturing but low on control, avoiding decisions on boundary-making or discipline. The authoritarian parent has a profile which uses high disciplinary and controlling techniques alongside low elements of warmth and responsiveness. This might be the parent whose

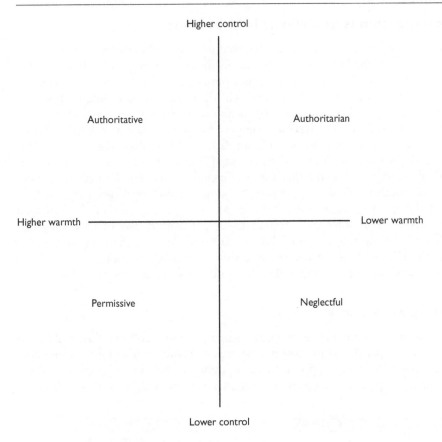

Figure 1.1 An adaptation of Maccoby and Martin (1983) and Baumrind's (1991) four
parenting styles.

strategy is to control through negative interactions: 'Stop that or you'll get a smack'....
Finally, the authoritative parent will maintain high levels of control and boundary
setting but this will be applied in a culture of warmth, and questioning, problem-solving
discussion, which fosters empathy and sympathy (Carlo *et al.*, 2010, p. 117).

A number of studies support this model, concurring that there are 'positive relations
between parental warmth and prosocial behaviour' (Janssens and Deković, 1997, p. 512)
In addition, Janssens and Deković's paper noted that 'a supportive, authoritative and less
restrictive child-rearing style was associated with a higher level of reasoning about moral
dilemmas, and with more prosocial behaviour'.

This could also be because discussions about moral dilemmas, in order to be internal-
ised and effective, would need to take place within an engagement which is supportive
and discursive and open to different interpretations. This may not be the case with an
authoritarian parent. In addition, the relationship with an authoritarian parent may be
tense and with undercurrents of anger and tension that might reduce a child's ability to
undertake effective perspective-taking (Carlo *et al.*, 2010, p. 116). Also, the child who
is threatened or disciplined with verbal or physical assault is likely to adopt the message
behind the punishment and emulate that behaviour (Kochanska *et al.*, 2003), thus
negating the message.

What partnership is and why it is important

Earlier on in this chapter, evidence was presented that establishes that working in partnership can support children's outcomes: the evidence is widespread. However, the development of partnership with parents is not only helpful for the unique children in settings but also has a value for wider society. The development of trusting relationships between practitioners and parents offers opportunities to receive support and information, which may lead to more intensive support for families if it is needed. Reports published by the Centre for Mental Health (Khan, 2014; Parsonage et al., 2014) demonstrate the impact of childhood behavioural difficulties on our society and on families. Childhood behavioural difficulties may include: 'persistent disobedience, angry outbursts and tantrums, physical aggression, fighting, destruction of property, stealing, lying and bullying' (Parsonage et al., 2014, p. 6). About 5 per cent of children aged 5–10 have a conduct disorder and a further 15–20 per cent 'display behavioural problems which fall below this threshold but are still serious enough to merit concern because of the increased risk of adverse outcomes in later life' (Parsonage et al., 2014, p. 6). The negative outcomes associated with conduct disorder are shown in Figure 1.2.

Supporting all parents

As professionals with regular and close contact with all parents who bring their children to settings, there are opportunities to support and signpost parents to other forms of intervention where needed. Parenting support is seen as a priority by the current government (DfE, 2012) and there are parenting programmes and interventions available to those who have

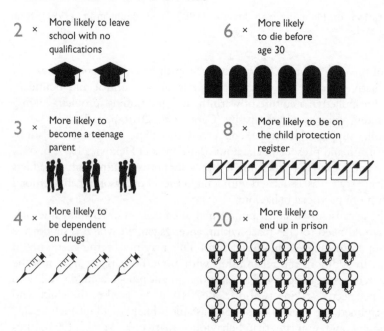

Figure 1.2 Negative outcomes associated with conduct disorder (Parsonage et al., 2014, p. 7).

specific support requirements. Additionally, supportive relationships in settings can build up trust and enable parents to share anxieties and concerns with key people in particular, which may be enough to secure stable and consistent behaviour patterns for children.

Referral

In early years settings, practitioners are able to identify emerging behavioural problems and, through building warm and supportive relationships with parents, based on support and strengths-based practice (see Chapter 7), it is possible to share ideas with parents to modify behaviour patterns and redress potential problems at an early stage.

Early years settings are a point of contact for parents that can offer support and referral options, possibly to parenting programmes. Not only can this help with modifying the behaviour of the child, but it can also reduce safeguarding issues. 'A large-scale study in the United States showed that the Triple P parenting programmes resulted in fewer instances of maltreatment and considerable reductions in child protection costs compared with areas where parents had no access to these programmes' (Khan, 2014, p. 11). The range of opportunities are wide: from advice on early literacy or teething, to listening and encouraging parents to invest in evidence-based parenting interventions, and there is a wide range of professionals working with children and families who build these relationships.

Chapter summary

The function of the family to regulate behaviour and promote prosocial, well-adjusted individuals who fit into society is supported to an increasing degree by the state. There is some debate that critiques the involvement of professional services in the raising of children, claiming that it disempowers parents:

> Professional intervention often involves putting parents in their place as inept amateurs. Occasionally it involves blaming parents for the problems they face. At the very least, professionals demand a privileged status for themselves as experts and make parents dependent on them.
>
> (Ferudi, 2008, p. 172)

Concurrently, the evidence that parental involvement is effective in child outcomes has led the sector to make increasing efforts to involve parents. Effective partnerships between early years practitioners and parents can offer support, signposting, ideas and strategies as well as improve children's lives. But parents have to trust us, and we may not be worthy of that trust if we mis-use the term partnership.

Next steps . . .

This chapter has looked at some of the issues facing parents and the practitioners who work with them. Being able to show empathy and understanding to parents can break down barriers and increase trust, both of which enable information to flow more freely between parent and practitioner. In order to do this, practitioners must demonstrate robust listening skills. This resource has a range of tutorials and activities intended to improve listening skills: www.learnhigher.ac.uk/working-with-others/listening-and-interpersonal-skills/listening-and-interpersonal-skills-tutorial/.

References

Ainsworth, M.D.L., Blehar, M.C., Waters, E. and Wall, S. (1978) *Patterns of Attachment: A Psychological Study of the Strange Situation*. Hillsdale, NJ: Erlbaum.

Asmussen, K. (2011) *The Evidence-based Parenting Practitioner's Handbook*. Abingdon: Routledge.

Bandura, A. (1977) *Social Learning Theory*. Englewood Cliffs, NY: Prentice Hall.

Bates, R.J. (2009) Building imperial youth? Reflections on labour and the construction of working-class childhood in late Victorian England. *Paedagogica Historica*, 45(1–2): 143–156.

Baumrind, D. (1991) The influence of parenting style on adolescence competence and substance use. *Journal of Early Adolescence*, 11: 56–95.

Bee, H. and Boyd, D. (2010) *The Developing Child*, 12th edition. Boston: Pearson Education.

Blanden, J. (2006) *'Bucking the Trend': What Enables Those Who Are Disadvantaged in Childhood to Succeed Later in Life?* A report of research carried out by the Department of Economics, University of Surrey and the Centre for Economic Performance, London School of Economics on behalf of the Department for Work and Pensions. Leeds: Department for Work and Pensions.

Bowlby, J. (1953) *Childcare and the Growth of Love*. London: Penguin.

Bowlby, J. (1997) *Attachment and Loss, V1: Attachment*. London: Hogarth Press.

Bronfenbrenner, U. (2005) *Making Human Beings Human: Bioecological Perspectives on Human Development*. London: Sage Publications.

Burnette, J. (2008) *Women Workers in the British Industrial Revolution*. EH.Net Encyclopedia, edited by Robert Whaples. 26 March 2008. Online: http://eh.net/encyclopedia/women-workers-in-the-british-industrial-revolution/ (accessed 26 July 2014).

Carlo, G., Mestre, M.V., Samper, P., Tur, A. and Armenter, B.E. (2010) The longitudinal relations among dimensions of parenting styles, sympathy, prosocial moral reasoning, and prosocial behaviours. *International Journal of Behavioral Development*, 35: 116–124.

Department for Education (DfE) (2010) *Parental Opinion Survey 2010. DfE-RR061*. London: DfE.

Department for Education (DfE) (2012) Prime Minister announces support for families. Online: www.gov.uk/government/news/prime-minister-announces-support-for-families--2 (accessed 28 July 2014).

Department for Education (DfE) (2014) *Early Years Foundation Stage: Statutory Framework*. London: DfE.

Department for Education and Skills (DfES) (2007) *Every Parent Matters*. Nottingham: DfES. Online: http://webarchive.nationalarchives.gov.uk/20091115062648/dcsf.gov.uk/everychild-matters/resources-and-practice/ig00219/ (accessed 8 April 2015).

Desforges, A. and Abouchaar, A. (2003) *The Impact of Parental Involvement, Parental Support and Family Education on Pupil Achievement and Adjustment: A Literature Review. DfES Report No 433*. DfES: Nottingham.

Elfer, P., Goldschmeid, E. and Selleck, D. (2003) *Key Persons in the Nursery: Building Relationships for Quality Provision*. London: David Fulton.

Ferudi, F. (2008) *Paranoid Parenting: Why Ignoring the Experts May Be Best for your Child*. London: Continuum Press.

Fuller, C. (2014) Social capital and the role of trust in aspirations for higher education. *Educational Review*, 66(2): 131–147.

Howe, D. (2011) *Attachments across the Lifecourse: A Brief Introduction*. Basingstoke: Palgrave Macmillan.

Janssens, J.M.A.M. and Deković, M. (1997) Child rearing, prosocial moral reasoning and prosocial behaviour. *International Journal of Behavioral Development*, 20(3): 509–527.

Khan, L. (2014) *Wanting the Best for My Children: Parents' Voices*. Report for Centre for Mental Health. London: Centre for Mental Health. Online: www.centreformentalhealth.org.uk/publications/wanting_the_best_for_my_children.aspx?ID=700 (accessed 28 July 2014).

Kochanska, G., Aksan, N. and Nichols, K.E. (2003) Maternal power assertion in discipline and moral discourse contexts: commonalities, differences, and implications for children's moral conduct and cognition. *Developmental Psychology*, 39: 949–963.

Maccoby, E.E. and Martin, J.A. (1983) Socialization in the context of the family: parent–child interaction. In E.M. Hetherington (ed.) *Handbook of Child Psychology: Socialization, Personality and Social Development, vol. 4.* New York: Wiley.

Mason, J. and Tipper, B. (2008) Being related: how children define and create kinship. *Childhood,* 15: 441–460.

Melhuish, E.C., Mai, B., Phan, M.P., Sylva, K., Sammons, P., Siraj-Blatchford, I. and Taggart, B. (2008) Effects of the home learning environment and preschool centre experience upon literacy and numeracy development in early primary school. *Journal of Social Issues,* 64(1): 95–114.

Muschamp, Y., Wikeley, F., Ridge, T. and Balarin, M. (2007) *Parenting, Caring and Educating. Primary Review Research Study 7/1.* Interim Report. Cambridge: University of Cambridge. Online: http://core.kmi.open.ac.uk/download/pdf/309511.pdf (accessed 15 December 2014).

Office for National Statistics (ONS) (2011) *Mothers in the Labour Market, 2011.* Online: www. ons.gov.uk/ons/dcp171776_234036.pdf (accessed 13 August 2014).

Panico, L., Bartley, M., Kelly, Y., McMunn, A. and Sacker, A. (2010) Changes in family structure in early childhood in the Millennium Cohort Study. *Population Trends,* 142: 75–89.

Parsonage, M., Khan, L. and Saunders, A. (2014) *Building a Better Future: The Lifetime Costs of Childhood Behavioural Problems and the Benefits of Early Intervention.* Report for Centre for Mental Health. London: Centre for Mental Health. Online: www.centreformentalhealth.org. uk/publications/building_a_better_future.aspx?ID=699 (accessed 28 July 2014).

Plowden, B. (1967) *Children and their Primary Schools: A Report of the Central Advisory Council for Education (England) (Plowden Report).* London: HMSO.

Qualifications and Curriculum Authority/Department for Education and Employment (2000) *Curriculum Guidance for the Foundation Stage.* London: QCA.

Rutter, M. (1987) Psychosocial resilience and protective mechanisms. *American Journal of Orthopsychiatry,* 57(3): 316–330.

Stewart, M., Reid, G. and Mangham, C. (1997) Fostering children's resilience. *Journal of Pediatric Nursing,* 12(1): 21–31.

Sylva, K., Melhuish, E., Sammons, P., Siraj-Blatchford, I. and Taggart, B. (2004) *The Effective Provision of Pre-school Education (EPPE) Project Final Report. A Longitudinal Evaluation (1997–2004).* London: DfES.

Vygotsky, L.(1978) *Mind in Society.* Cambridge, MA: Harvard University Press.

Yeo, A. and Lovell, T. (2003) *Sociology and Social Policy for the Early Years,* 2nd edition. London: Hodder and Stoughton.

Chapter 2

Introducing legislative and policy frameworks

In this chapter, we shall be looking at:

* relevant legislation in relation to working with parents
* relevant policy in relation to working with parents.

In a developed economy such as that in the UK, society is driven and managed within structures and frameworks, both local and national, formal and informal. These evolve over time, influenced by a number of factors, such as economic climate, prevailing beliefs, constituents of society and of course by the political parties who hold power, which in a democracy should broadly reflect the prevailing views of the population. The process of democratic change is implemented through legislation and so, in order to see the value which any part of society has within a given time, it can be helpful to look at the passage of legislation within that area of interest.

The current legislative landscape for parent partnership

The involvement of parents in education and care has been slow to evolve, as 'parents, the home, the community and schools were seen as completely separate units and did not encroach on each other's perceived roles or responsibilities' (Turner, 2014, p. 178).

But in the post-World War Two period, and especially from the 1960s onwards, it has been possible to see, through government policy, a growing understanding of the role of the parent, and the increasing recognition of the value of parental involvement and the home learning environment.

From Table 2.1, it is possible to see the legislative embedding of parental involvement from a peripheral aspect of children's education towards a more mainstream position with recognition of their influence on children's development.

The implementation of government policy relating to the collaboration between parents and educational practitioners has taken a more central role in the education and care of children since government-commissioned research identified the essential role of the family in children's outcomes. A slow but consistent trickle of evidence has endorsed the impact of parental involvement of parents (Desforges and Abouchaar, 2003; Sylva *et al.*, 2004).

The pace of change has increased steadily with policy changes that recognise that the role of the parent, carer or family has an important role to play in developing both the relationship between school and home, and the outcomes of those children in terms of development and academic attainment.

Table 2.1 Examples of legislation and policy regarding parental involvement in children's education

1967	Plowden Report – this report emphasised the importance of home/school communication and Parent Teacher Associations (Plowden, 1967).
1978	The Warnock Report on special educational needs recognised the contribution of parents and also their need for support (Warnock, 1978).
1988	The Education Reform Act introduced the National Curriculum and, through the application of a more market-led philosophy, gave parents more access to information and governance, seeing them and their children as consumers of the education 'service'.
1989	The Children Act – this consolidating Act placed parents firmly within a partnership model in terms of safeguarding and working with professionals. So whilst not specifically related to education, the principles of the Act aimed to give parents more visibility within the decision-making process. The principles state that: • the best interests of the child are paramount • parents should be encouraged to work in partnership with agencies, participating in the processes of decisions relating to their child • delays are detrimental to children's welfare.
1996	The Education Act – gave parents a louder voice in matters of choices for mainstreaming schooling for children with special educational needs and disabilities. It also placed more responsibilities on schools to involve parents in decisions in relation to their children.
2001	Special Education Needs and Disability Act and SEN Code of Practice provided 'practical advice to Local Education Authorities, maintained schools, early education settings and others on carrying out their statutory duties to identify, assess and make provision for children's special educational needs' (DfES, 2001, p. iii). The 2001 Code of Practice contains a complete chapter devoted to working in partnership with parents.
2003	Green Paper: Every Child Matters. The purpose of the Every Child Matters (ECM) agenda was to recognise that children and young people 'cannot learn if they do not feel safe or if health problems create barriers' (Cheminais, 2006, p. 1) and that the most effective method to ensure the ECM outcomes was to ensure not only a multi-agency perspective but also one which supported the principles of parent partnership. The Every Child Matters agenda was enshrined in law through the Children Act 2004.
2004	The Children Act 2004 was passed in response to a number of safeguarding issues and its purpose was to increase the safety of children through an increase in multi-agency working and also taking into account the important role of parents and carers.
2006	The Childcare Act of 2006 provided the legal framework and the delivery requirements for the change in the English and Welsh education and care policy which was the Early Years Foundation Stage (DCSF, 2008). The framework was a combination of the Foundation Stage of 3–5 years (Qualifications and Curriculum Authority, 2000) and the Birth to Three Matters framework (Department for Education and Skills, 2003). There was specific guidance in the EYFS (DSCF, 2008; DfE 2012 and 2014) on the role of the key person, and there was a requirement to 'share relevant information with each other and with parents' (DCSF, 2007, p. 10).
2014	Children and Families Act implemented the new Special Educational Needs Code of Practice – giving parents wider powers to make decisions in relation to children's special needs.

From the deficit view of parents to the development of a multi-agency model of working where the family sits at the centre of supporting services, it is easy to think that the progression is one-directional. However, the effects of the global economic crisis of the past six years has resulted in many policies being in place but few resources being available to action them. So whilst the rhetoric of support is maintained, the direction is more targeted than universal, with reduced funding to local authorities preventing them from supporting their settings through professional development.

Activity

Ask friends, family and colleagues who were under five during the 1960s or 1970s about who looked after them before they started school. Find out whether they remember parents being involved in the schools and, if so, in what particular way.

Recent policy and value drivers of working with parents

Legislation such as that in Table 2.1 (especially the more recent changes) has been asso-ciated with a range of reviews which have explored the ways that families are supported and the impact of a range of factors (including the home learning environment) on children's well-being and developmental outcomes. These reviews include those shown in Table 2.2.

Table 2.2 Reviews on the role of parents in their children's development and learning

2003	Desforges and Abouchaar – literature review on parental involvement. *Effective Provision of Pre-School Education Research* (Sylva et al., 2004) Both of these major documents evidenced the impact of the role of parents in a number of ways that contributed to children's outcomes.
2007	*Children's Plan and Building Brighter Futures* – in their policy document, the Labour Party asserted that: 'schools need to become better at working with parents', 'government does not bring up children – parents do' (Department for Children, Schools and Families, 2007, p. 4). This demonstrates their commitment to the autonomy of the family and the balance of power within the professional/parent relationship.
2010	F. Field, *The Foundation Years: Preventing Poor Children Becoming Poor Adults.* Field's review was one of a number of publications at this time which highlighted the importance of supporting parents because of the significance of their role.
2011	Graham Allen, *Early Intervention – The Next Steps.* This document reinforced the message that: 'What parents do is more important than who they are. Especially in a child's earliest years, the right kind of parenting is a bigger influence on their future than wealth, class, education or any other common social factor' (Allen, 2011, p. xiv).
2014	Reviewed by Dame Clare Tickell, the revised Early Years Foundation Stage (DfE, 2014) reinforced the importance of the 'role of parents and carers as partners in their children's learning' (Tickell, 2011, p. 5).
2014	Cross-party manifesto: *The 1,001 Critical Days: The Importance of the Conception to Age Two Period.* In this document, it is stated that: 'The health and early years workforce should receive high quality training in infant mental health and attachment as standard, in order for practitioners to understand parent–infant relationships and the services required when difficulties arise. Specialist training should include identifying the 5–7% most seriously ill and at-risk parents' (Leadsom et al., 2013, p. 9).

Professional frameworks

As the culture of cooperation and communication has become more clearly established, so the sector has also provided practitioners with guidelines and frameworks to support practice and also to encourage collaborative professional practice across the range of professionals working in the Children's Workforce. The purpose of this has been to try to increase cooperative working through a more shared language and dialogue.

The Work with Parents National Occupational Standards

The National Occupational Standards for working with parents were originally drafted in 2005 and further developed in 2010. They are one of a number of occupational standards. The final version of the National Occupational Standards for working with parents was published in 2011 (Lifelong Learning UK, 2011) and its purpose is to offer an overview of the competences used by a range of professionals who work with parents. This range of professionals includes psychologists, therapists, parenting practitioners, educational assistants and youth workers, so of course the standards do not represent all the work of all those working with parents. For example, some will relate directly to those who work as parenting practitioners, delivering programmes to parents, whereas other workers will have a less direct involvement.

For the purposes of this book, the most useful elements of the National Occupational Standards are the principles and values, as these can be used for reflection on what we do and how we do it. The following principles and values underpin the Work with Parents sector (Lifelong Learning UK, 2011):

- All work with parents should reflect the rights of the child set out in the UN Convention on the Rights of the Child (UNICEF, 1989) ratified by the UK in December 1991.
- Practitioners need to work in partnership with parents at all times, encouraging independence and self-reliance.
- Mothers, fathers and those in a parenting role are acknowledged as having unique knowledge and information about their children and are the primary educators of their children.
- Children are the responsibility of, and make a positive contribution to, the wider society as well as their families.
- Work with parents should value and build on parents' existing strengths, knowledge and experience.
- Parenting information, education, support and interventions should be available to, and practitioners should engage with, all those in a parenting role.
- Services should aim to offer a range of appropriate support according to both child and parent level of need, and what is available in the family already and in communities.
- Respect for diversity and different needs, promotion of equality and taking action to overcome threatening, offensive or discriminatory behaviour and attitudes are of fundamental importance to work with parents.
- Anyone who works with parents should have specific training, qualifications and expertise that are appropriate to the work they are undertaking.
- Good practice requires reflection, regular and appropriate supervision and support as well as a continuing search for improvement.

- Parenting practitioners utilise effective working partnerships with agencies and individuals in providing support to parents and families. Integrated working and the sharing of approaches across services is a key element of this role.
- Parenting information, education, support and interventions should utilise the best known evidence for good outcomes for children and parents.
- Parenting practitioners should be committed to engaging with children, young people and families fully through identifying goals, assessing options, mentoring or coaching, making decisions and reviewing outcomes. They should support children's and families' involvement in the development, delivery and evaluation of children's services.
- Work with parents should place the interests of children and young people at the heart of the work. Practitioners are committed to working with parents and families so that children and young people have the opportunity to achieve positive outcomes.
- Work with parents recognises the need for innovation and creativity to address both emerging and local needs and to build self-regulating and supportive community networks.

(Lifelong Learning UK, 2011)

Activity

Choose one of the principles and values above. Consider the work that you are doing with parents and reflect upon the ways in which your work reflects this principle. If there are areas that you feel you can build on, explore the ways in which you might do this. You could link up with other students or practitioners and develop presentations, based on the principles above. We shall explore these more in the next chapter.

Common Core of Skills and Knowledge for the Children's Workforce

The Common Core 'describes the skills and knowledge that everyone who works with children and young people is expected to have' (CWDC, 2010, p. 2). Within its six sections is one entitled 'Effective communication and engagement with children, young people and families'. The purpose of the document is to demonstrate the transferability of the skills used across the Children's Workforce, but also to give practitioners a set of standards against which to measure one's own performance (through reflection) or to use it as a training or audit tool within settings. It includes the key concepts of trust-building, active listening, respect, empathy, honesty and understanding of cultural and other contexts.

Principles for Engaging with Families

Whilst the previous two frameworks have broad guidance principles in relation to those working within the EYFS and also the Children's Workforce, the next framework gives specific guidance to working with families. The *Principles for Engaging with Families* document can be found in full on the internet (NCB:ELPPEG, 2010), but the principles are given here:

Successful and sustained engagement with families

1 ...is maintained when practitioners work alongside families in a valued working relationship
2 ...involves practitioners and parents being willing to listen to and learn from each other
3 ...happens when practitioners respect what families know and already do
4 ...needs practitioners to find ways to actively engage those who do not traditionally access services
5 ...happens when families are decision-makers in organisations and services
6 ...happens when families' views, opinions and expectations of services are raised and their confidence increases as service users
7 ...happens where there is support for the whole family
8 ...is through universal services but with opportunities for more intensive support where most needed
9 ...requires effective support and supervision for staff, encouraging evaluation and self-reflection
10 ...requires an understanding and honest sharing of issues around safeguarding.

(NCB:ELPPEG, 2010)

Parents, Early Years and Learning Activities

Finally, the PEAL project (Parents, Early Years and Learning Activities) (Wheeler and Connor, 2006) produced another set of values.

Values underpinning the PEAL programme

The terms mothers and fathers and parents, when used here, refer to all the male and female adults who are in a primary carer role in a child's life.

- Children learn best in the context of warm, loving relationships.
- Parents play the key role in children's learning. They are experts on their own children and they are a child's first and enduring educators.
- Parents want the best for their children and want to be involved in their children's learning.
- All parents are entitled to be involved in children's learning and to be supported in whatever way they are able or wish to engage.
- All families and individual children are different, and acknowledging and respecting this is crucial to building genuine relationships built on trust and openness.
- Life for young children isn't separated into education and care times and places, play times or learning times. It is a seamless whole, whether they are in their homes or in early years provision; and the importance of this continuity should be reflected in settings and in other family support services.

(Wheeler and Connor, 2006, p. 20)

> **Activity**
>
> Compare and contrast the different values bases. What are the similarities and differences?

Early Years Teacher Status

Graduate level qualifications for those working with infants and young children in pre-school settings have developed since the EPPE findings (Sylva, 2004) evidenced the impact of qualified staff on children's outcomes. Since then, Early Years Professionals/Early Years Teachers, lead practice in many settings. The qualification does not confer Qualified Teacher Status on its holders. The current EYT Standards can be found in Appendix 1.

Conclusion

So we know who works with parents, we know about the policy and legislative framework which regulates their practice and we now know more about the theoretical framework which informs practice and legislation. There is a consistency in the positioning of all these aspects.

Poverty is a prime determinant of poor outcomes and, throughout this textbook, reference will be made to the ways in which poverty has a pernicious effect on children in society. There are ways that we can use our power and skills to improve children's chances of escape from poverty through education and resilience. Blanden states:

> The most robust result found is that parental interest in child's education is very important. This implies that parenting interventions such as Sure Start could have an important long-term effect if they encourage parents to become more involved in their children's education.
>
> (Blanden, 2006, p. 25)

Is it really only settings such as Sure Start that can maintain this work? As practitioners who are working with parents at all times, are we missing a trick?

> **Next steps...**
>
> Parents who come to settings may be eligible for government support in a range of ways. It is possible that they are not aware of all the support they can access. One starting point is the government website: www.gov.uk/browse/benefits/families.
>
> One current benefit is 'Care to Learn' (bearing in mind that this may not be in place after the General Election), which can help with childcare costs for parents who are under 20 and in study. Find out more about this (www.gov.uk/care-to-learn) and consider the ways that your setting helps the community to gain qualifications and support.

References

Allen, G. (2011) *Early Intervention: The Next Steps. An Independent Report to Her Majesty's Government*. London: HM Government.

Blanden, J. (2006) *'Bucking the Trend': What Enables Those Who Are Disadvantaged in Childhood to Succeed Later in Life?* A report of research carried out by the Department of Economics, University of Surrey and the Centre for Economic Performance, London School of Economics on behalf of the Department for Work and Pensions. Leeds: Department for Work and Pensions.

Cheminais, R. (2006) *Every Child Matters: A Practical Guide for Teachers*. Abingdon: David Fulton.

Children's Workforce Development Council (CWDC) (2010) *The Common Core of Skills and Knowledge for the Children and Young People's Workforce*. Leeds: CWDC. Online: http://webarchive.nationalarchives.gov.uk/20120119192332/http://cwdcouncil.org.uk/assets/0000/9297/CWDC_CommonCore7.pdf (accessed 17 August 2014).

Department for Children, Schools and Families (DCSF) (2007) *The Children's Plan*. London: DCSF.

Department for Children, Schools and Families (DCSF) (2008) *Statutory Framework for the Early Years Foundation Stage*. Nottingham: DCSF Publications

Department for Education (DfE) (2012) *Early Years Foundation Stage: Statutory Framework*. London: DfE.

Department for Education (DfE) (2014) *Early Years Foundation Stage: Statutory Framework*. London: DfE.

Department for Education and Skills (DfES) (2001) *Special Educational Needs Code of Practice*. London: DfES.

Department for Education and Skills (DfES) (2003) *Birth to Three Matters Framework*. Nottingham: DfES.

Desforges, C. and Abouchaar, A. (2003) *The Impact of Parental Involvement, Parental Support and Family Education on Pupil Achievements and Adjustment: A Literature Review*, RR433. Nottingham: DfES.

Field, F. (2010) *The Foundation Years: Preventing Poor Children Becoming Poor Adults: The Report of the Independent Review on Poverty and Life Chances*. London: HM Government.

Leadsom, A., Field, F., Burstow, P. and Lucas, C. (2013). *The 1,001 Critical Days: The Importance of the Conception to Age Two Period: A Cross-Party Manifesto*. London: DH.

Lifelong Learning UK (2011) *National Occupational Standards for Work with Parents*. Online: http://pelorous.totallyplc.com/media_manager/public/115/publications/Qualifications/work-with-parents-nos-jan-2011.pdf (accessed 17 August 2014).

National Children's Bureau (NCB): Early Learning Partnership Parental Engagement Group (2010) *Principles for Engaging with Families: A Framework for Local Authorities and National Organisations to Evaluate and Improve Engagement with Families*. London: NCB/National Quality Improvement Network. Online: www.ncb.org.uk/media/236258/engaging_with_families.pdf (accessed 8 April 2014).

National College for Teaching and Leadership (NCTL) (2013) *Teachers' Standards (Early Years) From September 2013*. London: NCTL.

Plowden, B. (1967) *Children and their Primary Schools: A Report of the Central Advisory Council for Education (England)* (Plowden Report). London: HMSO.

Qualifications and Curriculum Authority (2000) *Curriculum Guidance for the Foundation Stage*. London: QCA.

Sylva, K., Melhuish, E., Sammons, P., Siraj-Blatchford, I. and Taggart, B. (2004) *The Effective Provision of Pre-school Education (EPPE) Project Final Report. A Longitudinal Evaluation (1997–2004)*. London: DfES.

Tickell, Dame C. (2011) *The Early Years: Foundations for Life, Health and Learning*. London: DfE.

Turner, D. (2014) Parents, carers and the community: the collaborative relationship. In S. Brownhill (ed.) *Empowering the Children's and Young People's Workforce: Practice Based Knowledge, Skills and Understanding*. Abingdon: Routledge.

UNICEF (1989) *UN Convention on the Rights of the Child*. Geneva: UN.

Warnock Report (1978) *Special Educational Needs. Report of the Committee of Enquiry into the Education of Handicapped Children and Young People*. London: HMSO. Online: www.educationengland.org.uk/documents/warnock/warnock1978.html (accessed 13 August 2014).

Wheeler, H. and Connor, J. (2006) *Parents, Early Years and Learning Activities*. London: National Children's Bureau.

Chapter 3

The importance of reflection

In this chapter, we shall be looking at:

* linking between the personal and professional in relation to parenting
* reflection and key reflective theorists
* constructs of parenting and parenting practice and the practitioner experience.

Introduction and links to Early Years Teachers' Standards (NCTL, 2013)

Early years practitioners work within a culture of reflection, developing strategies, both in their roles as professionals and through their professional and academic training, to learn from their work-based experiences. Reflective practice is a requirement of the Early Years Teachers' Standards (National College for Teaching and Leadership [NCTL], 2013) which requires that early years teachers are able to:

> Reflect on the effectiveness of teaching activities and educational programmes to support the continuous improvement of provision.
>
> (Standard 4.5)

> Reflect on and evaluate the effectiveness of provision, and shape and support good practice.
>
> (Standard 8.6)

The Early Years Teachers' (EYT) Standards document emphasises the importance of the role of working with parents: 'They forge positive professional relationships and work with parents and/or carers in the best interests of babies and children' (NCTL, 2013, p. 2). In addition, they emphasise the important relationship between family and setting. For example, early years teachers should:

> Know when a child is in need of additional support and how this can be accessed, working in partnership with parents and/or carers and other professionals.
>
> (Standard 5.5)

> Engage effectively with parents and/or carers and other professionals in the on-going assessment and provision for each child.
>
> (Standard 6.2)

Give regular feedback to children and parents and/or carers to help children progress towards their goals.

(Standard 6.3)

Linking between the personal and professional in relation to parenting

Graduate-led settings work within these Standards in order to build relationships with families, but building constructive and warm relationships with parents and carers does require considerable reflection upon personal values and previous experiences, which is where reflective practice can be used as a tool to support professionalism.

Throughout our lives, our cognitive processes help us to categorise experiences. Our own experiences and memories define our own realities and therefore events that digress from there may seem negative, deficient or unsuitable, even though in reality they are simply different. An example of this may be the alternate ways that parents manage their children's behaviour, such as bedtime routines or discipline.

Activity

We all bring values with us in our personal and professional lives. Every individual has a set of values, whether implicit or explicit. They are used when goals are set, decisions are made, opinions are formed. Think of three values that you hold. The following case study may help you to generate ideas.

Case Study[1]

Sarah decided that her three important values were honesty, good manners and the importance of human rights. When she thought about where they came from, she realised that her mum had always taught her to tell the truth when she was a child, and if her mum was cross with her for doing something wrong, she knew that she would be less cross than if she found out she had been lying! Then she remembered that her primary school used golden rules where everyone was encouraged to be kind to each other and say please and thank you and she remembered how much she liked it when someone said thank you to her. Finally, when she completed her early years qualification, she learned about children's rights and how important they were so she maintained that she would always work towards all children enjoying basic rights. Through her course and talking to other students, she developed a belief that just because children are younger does not mean they should not enjoy the freedoms and entitlements that rights can bring.

- Notice where your values have come from – your family? Community or cultural beliefs beyond your family? Your own experiences? Think about whether you have discarded some values that you had as a child, but kept others. Why? Share in pairs – notice similarities and differences.
- Try to think beyond describing your values, but really work out why these values were, or are, important to you.
- Also consider whether you found it easy to dismiss the values that are embedded within your family or culture. Sometimes values are so much part of a family that it is difficult to look at them objectively.

The importance of reflection

What is reflection?

The review of experience is part of reflection, but that is only the beginning of the process. Jenny Moon works in this area and she has developed a technique of writing what she calls 'graduated scenarios' (Moon, 2009) to illustrate the degree of personal learning that can be gained from reflection. Here is an example (not written by Moon, but written in the same developmental style) of a graduated scenario, which tells the same story more than once, and with each re-telling of the story, the thinking and reflection is widened and developed. The first narration is quite descriptive, but the second and especially the third rendering of the story allows the speaker to reflect more widely, to look at the perspectives of others and to consider future actions based on the reflections. Read the scenarios through once or twice, and then note what is description and what is reflection in each of them. In that way, you will be able to see how description is only a small part of reflection.

Part one

I was in the school office last week – it was the week before half term so there was lots going on: teachers wanting to arrange meetings during half term; support staff collecting permission slips; children with money to hand in for the school trip coming up at Easter and two of the trainee teachers who were doing placements in years 1 and 2. They were doing some photocopying – probably it was the PowerPoint slides of the talk that was given to staff yesterday concerning changes in safeguarding policies. The two of them have hooked up together and seem to get on very well, which helps them as they get an extra layer of support from each other. They come from different training providers so I expect they found it useful to compare notes on the experiences they were having this year.

As all this was taking place, I heard one member of staff talking to another. It was about one of the families whose children come to the school. Although no names were mentioned at first, it was obvious to me who they were talking about – and probably to everyone else in the room. But no-one said anything, just got on with what they were doing.

The member of staff was talking about an incident that had happened in the playground and she wanted to remember the second name of one of the children in year 1. She said, 'Can you tell me the surname of Mikey in Acorns Class? You know...' and then she lowered her voice and said, laughing, '...Mikey the pikey!'

I must say that it did make me feel uncomfortable. I don't think that it should have been said where children can hear. And I know that when you first come into a setting, you look up to everyone and assume they know better than you. But really, that comment wasn't appropriate. Perhaps I should have picked up on it at the time, but I was being observed and knew that I needed to spend the lunchtime tidying up my planning and finishing the flash cards I was going to use. And then the moment passed and there seemed no point in dragging it up again after half term.

Part two

I was in the school office last week – it was the week before half term so there was lots going on, with teachers and support staff, children and two trainee teachers all in there. As all this was taking place, I heard one member of staff talking to another. It was about one of the families whose children come to the school. Although no names were mentioned at first, it was obvious to me who they were talking about – and probably to everyone else in the room. But no-one said anything. I wonder whether they were all like me – a bit too surprised to speak.

The member of staff was talking about an incident that had happened in the playground and she wanted to remember the second name of one of the children in year 1. She said, 'Can you tell me the surname of Mikey in Acorns Class? You know…' and then she lowered her voice and said, laughing, '…Mikey the pikey!'

I could see that it was only meant as a joke, and it's something that everybody says – almost part of the language – a bit like the expression 'gay' really; and I know this super-visor is very professional and experienced, but I must say that it did make me feel uncomfortable. I don't think that it should have been said where children can hear – and trainee teachers for that matter. The fact that it was a member of staff almost legitimised it – if she says it then there's really no harm in it, is there? I know that when you first come into a setting, you look up to everyone and assume they know better than you. But really, that comment wasn't appropriate. Perhaps I should have picked up on it at the time. I thought about it afterwards and wondered why I didn't. And then the moment passed and there seemed no point in dragging it up again after half term. After all, there was little that could be done so long after the event, really. I did feel rather guilty though, that we had all condoned the negative message without really intending to.

Part three

I was in the school office last week – it was the week before half term so there was lots going on, with teachers, support staff, children and two trainee teachers all milling about. As all this was taking place, I heard one member of staff talking to another. It was about one of the families whose children come to the school. Although no names were men-tioned, it was obvious who they were talking about to me – and probably to everyone else in the room, but no-one said anything. I wonder whether they were all like me – a bit too surprised to speak.

The member of staff was talking about an incident that had happened in the playground and she wanted to remember the second name of one of the children in year 1. She said, 'Can you tell me the surname of Mikey in Acorns Class? You know…' and then she lowered her voice and said, laughing, '…Mikey the pikey!'

I got the impression that it was only meant as a joke, but it made me think about how funny Mikey's family would have found it. Looking around, I also noted the expression on the faces of the other members of the staff – open shock was imprinted on them, and this did not surprise me because here was an experienced member of staff, condoning the use of discriminatory language. It was impossible not to consider the effect of this on less senior members of staff, and on the children who were still in the room. The person who said it could be seen as a role model and therefore her behaviour was even more important because of social learning theory and how people are influenced by those that they respect.

Later that day, I started reflecting upon use of language – the word 'gay' is, for many of the younger generation, synonymous with silly, stupid, useless. My children use it in that way, but this incident made me really consider how it might feel to be gay, or a traveller, and to hear words linked to your identity being used negatively. It is, at best, thoughtless, and at worst, humiliating and confrontational – I can recall childhood days when racist slang was used much more freely. Those were the days of thoughtless racism, before the introduction of the 1976 Race Relations Act, with TV programmes such as the *Black and White Minstrel Show* being accepted without question. I feel relieved to live in a world which is more 'PC' because there is no doubt that society is more sensitive to insults and taunts, and indeed is required to heed relevant legislation in order to demonstrate anti-discriminatory practice to minority groups.

It seemed to be that the others in the room were embarrassed but said nothing. They left shortly after. The children may or may not have picked up on the comments. The fact that they were made within earshot indicates that this could happen again though, and it felt that the comment was made through negligence and stereotyping rather than racial hatred. However, the discomfort that seemed to swallow up the room indicated to me that we all felt uncomfortable about the interlude, but weren't quite sure how to deal with it.

I don't think that it should have been said where children can hear – and trainee teachers for that matter. The fact that it was a member of staff almost legitimised it – if she says it then there's really no harm in it, is there? I know that when you first come into a setting, you look up to everyone and assume they know better than you. But really, that comment not only wasn't appropriate, but sends a worrying message that language such as this is OK. So perhaps I should have picked up on it at the time. I thought about it afterwards and wondered why I didn't. It became clear to me that this should have been challenged and, as I reflected, it felt as though it should have been my job. But then the moment had passed and there seemed no point in dragging it up again after half term.

That was what I thought when I put it to the back of my mind, but when I really reflected upon it, I knew that there was a point to challenging it, but I really didn't want to because it would have been uncomfortable for me. But the more I thought about it, the more I decided that there was an important principle at stake. I could leave it, but that would be noted by other members of staff, who would also feel that they could 'leave it'. I also felt that the children may have heard the comment so there should be some input to the children as a whole, challenging the language. But how might I approach this? Could I really challenge her, and how would she respond? Angry, insulted, embarrassed, defensive? I decided that the best option was to talk to my line manager, in confidence, and without disclosing names, about the incident. Together, we agreed that this should be used as an opportunity to produce some positive messages about inclusion within the school, which would be applied to staff and children. By doing this, we could raise the issues and encourage all those in the school to consider the language they use without thinking.

If something like this happens again, I hope that I will be able to challenge it, but I also hope that the training that we are all embarking upon will help us all to become a little more inclusive and respectful of difference.

So, reflection includes a critical element; thinking beyond what actually happened, to why it happened and what has been learned. Jennie Lindon, describes it as 'thoughtfulness about one's own practice' (2010, p. 2) and, whilst that is the case, the element to explore is what thoughtfulness is. It can be harder to write (rather than speak) reflectively, and though many people may think reflectively, it can be hard to capture the part of it that is reflective. Reflection requires honesty and objectivity in order to have value. It indicates an openness to ongoing learning, rather than a defensiveness about situations. The advantage of it is that it can clarify confusion and help to identify opportunities for development and a greater self-awareness. The benefit of reflection is not just from the process though, but it is from what is learned from knowledge and self-awareness.

Key reflective theorists

John Dewey's reflective thinking

As an American philosopher and educationalist, John Dewey (1859–1952) explored the relationship between reflective thinking and learning (Dewey, 1909). His main beliefs and principles revolved around child-centred learning, and using the knowledge of the child, through use of observations and real experiences, to support learning.

Dewey's description of reflection in 1909 is a solid starting point to present-day reflection:

* 'Each phase is a step from something to something' (Dewey, 1909, p. 3).
* Reflective thought: 'active, persistent, and careful consideration of any belief or supposed form of knowledge in the light of the grounds that support it, and the further conclusions to which it tends' (Dewey, 1909, p. 6).

Dewey's process of reflection

1   We recognise that a problem or thought-provoking event has happened.
2   We try to interpret the event using existing knowledge and understanding.
3   We use our intelligence and skills to describe and explain the event thoroughly.
4   We use our thoughts from stage three to change our perceptions and expectations.
5   We alter our approach or thinking in order to improve or change things.

(Dewey, 1933, cited in Dryden *et al.*, 2005, p. 5)

So reflection can be seen as a combination of activities. Dewey defines it as an action that takes time (persistent), and where there is a clear intention to review events. Dewey believed that reflection is not something that happens without conscious thought and experience.

Reflection-in-action and reflection-on-action

Another pioneer of reflective practice, the US-based social scientist Donald Schön (1930–97), examined the ways that professionals from a range of disciplines used both reflection-in-action and reflection-on-action. He believed that the application of reflection-in-action was a method of problem-solving used extensively in professional practice, which required a 'feel' for the right action: 'you are noticing, at the very least, that you have been doing something right, and your "feeling" allows you to do that something again' (Schön, 1983, p. 55). Note the use of the word 'experienced'. Practitioners using reflection-in-action have accumulated experience upon which to base their decisions. They spontaneously use their knowledge and apply it to a current situation. The experience must be in position in the first place. This is why one might see a senior practitioner make decisions based on their knowledge of what they have learned works well.

On the other hand, reflection-on-action is the use of reflection to explore an experience, incident or event after it has taken place. It might take place whilst having a discussion within supervision, or perhaps when writing up a reflective log.

However, having an openness to the rationale for our decisions and the experience upon which they are based helps us to review assumptions too, which is an essential element of professionalism. In the next section on reflective practice, the use of espoused beliefs will be considered. The case study of June gives a useful example of what espoused beliefs are and also links to Johari's window and the gaps in June's knowledge.

What is espoused theory?

Espoused theory is the way that we perceive ourselves to work within certain principles, such as inclusion, child-centred approach and reflectiveness. Our espoused theory is the one we believe that we act upon. So, as June (see case study below) genuinely believed that her approach was inclusive of parents, this was her espoused theory.

> When someone is asked how he would behave under certain circumstances, the answer he usually gives is his espoused theory of action for that situation. This is the theory of action to which he gives allegiance, and which, upon request, he communicates to others. However, the theory that actually governs his actions is this theory-in-use.
>
> (Argyris and Schön, 1974, pp. 6–7)

Case study

June has been working as an early years practitioner for ten years. She has positive relationships with the parents she works with and she only has one-to-one meetings with parents who ask for this during the term. There is an annual parents' evening but that is not for another six months. From experience, she has learned that a small number of parents tell her when they want to meet up in private with her before then. Surinne and Sandip, however, know how busy June is, and don't want to trouble her with a private meeting, even though they are concerned about some of the behaviour their child is displaying. June has no idea that they would like to talk to her in private and Surinne and Sandip do not want to talk about this issue at the end of the day, in public. In terms of her practice, June uses her experience of practice to note that parents like her and relate to her well.

Then Maya, another parent, takes June aside when Surinne is collecting her son, and mentions a couple of issues that she does not want to discuss in the open. Maya is assertive and open and June is surprised to hear her need for privacy, but that induces a reflection-in-action and she asks everyone, as they are leaving, to contact her and she will make an appointment to meet up with them.

She then goes home and reflects further on this decision (reflection-on-action), reads up in some texts about the importance of offering parents regular meetings or phone calls and plans to raise this at the next staff meeting. She has been prepared to review her own beliefs and adapt her practice in order to meet the needs of parents to the best of her ability.

So, if June was asked what her approach to working with parents was, she might reply that she is available and works positively with them, and she has no reason to think otherwise, because nobody complains. And that is because the people who are being excluded are less assertive and therefore don't complain. So one can suggest that June's 'espoused theory' (Argyris and Schön, 1974) is that she has a collaborative relationship with all parents, but her theory in use is not so inclusive.

Maintaining objectivity through reflection and evidence-based practice

So, reflection can be used by professionals to explore actions and practice, in order to question our own motivations and assumptions and whether we actually use our espoused theories – or 'practice what we preach'. It is a way of gathering evidence and data – our own research on an issue. It is important that reflection is objective, looking at an issue from a range of perspectives and in a way that aids understanding rather than entrenches stereotypes. The use and application of theory to practice is an important element of reflection as, without the empirical data to consider against the personal data, there can be few conclusions drawn or learning opportunities taken. Evidence-based practice is part of this as it 'comprises a combination of research evidence ... respect for client values and practitioner expertise' (Asmussen, 2011, p. 29).

Using frameworks to support reflection

Reflection depends upon the practitioner spending less time on the description of the event that they wish to reflect upon and more time spent on the critical analysis of the event and the subsequent identification of learning that has taken place and which can be transposed onto new experiences. One might say that reflection as a skill is a difficult one to learn alone, as the interaction of a partner or mentor might support new understandings and development, much as a counsellor might challenge their client in order to extend thinking and challenge assumptions.

One way of facilitating reflection is through the use of reflective frameworks, such as those developed by Gibbs (1988), Johns (1994) and Jennifer Moon (2003). Figure 3.1 and the following text show summary points of Gibbs' (1988) and Johns' (1994) models of reflection. Take a look at them and research other frameworks for reflection.

Reflection is:

> 'Thinking about what you do and how'.
>
> (Lindon, 2010, p. 5)

Johns' model of structured reflection (1994)

Core question: What information do I need to access in order to learn through this experience?

Cue questions:

1   Description of the experience
2   Reflection
3   Influencing factors
4   Could I have dealt with the situation better?
5   Learning

Reflective activities

The use of these models can guide your reflections but, before you start, consider the ways in which you reflect. Do you find it easier to reflect in your head, or do you feel that you get more out of the experience if you also write it down? Do you find the

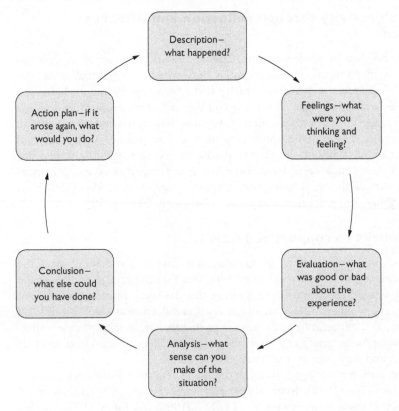

Figure 3.1 Reflective cycle (Gibbs, 1988).

most effective way to reflect is to work with colleagues and use shared experiences to reflect upon?

Perhaps you work with others, or you have a mentor, so you are able to talk through your experiences and can explore them in some depth with others. So, you may reflect in your head, perhaps as you are working and then maybe on the way home too. Or you may reflect with others, using colleagues as a sounding board and as an opportunity to develop further ideas. Alternatively, you may find that writing it down, perhaps within a reflective framework, gives your thoughts more permanence and enables you to develop strategies.

Activity

- Use the reflective model of your choice to consider a professional dilemma.
- Work with a partner and discuss aspects of that dilemma, and especially consider how your actions impact on your professional development.
- Consider your theories-in-use and espoused theories and the ways in which your practice influences your professional identity.
- Identify areas for change and areas in which you feel satisfied.
- Use the reflective model to frame your thoughts and consider next steps.
- Alternatively, capture your thoughts through developing your own model – drawn, written, spoken – whatever works best for you.

Reflecting on working with parents

From the perspective of longer term outcomes for children, the early years is a time to build relationships with families, in their first settings, establishing positive relationships built on trust, equality and respect, as the default position that all those involved in the care of young children can come to expect. For it is not just these early years that benefit from parent–practitioner engagement: 'Educators at all school levels know that successful students – at all ability levels – have families who stay informed and involved in their children's education' (Epstein, 2008, p. 9). However, many parents have negative associations related to the experiences of their own education which renders them reluctant to engage with figures in authority in education. This is only one of the many barriers that prevent relationships from blossoming (see Chapter 9 for more discussion on barriers).

Personal construct theory

For most practitioners, working with children will also mean working with parents, carers and, often, wider families. When thinking about that, how might you assume that the practitioner imagines those families to be? It would be patronising to think that they would all have a picture of families the same as their own, with the same ethnic background and the same socio-economic status. However, our brains have been collecting data, doing its own research, since we were born, and there are many assumptions that we make, based on what we have seen, read and heard (Kelly, 1955). Personal construct theory is the way that we make sense of the world, and it summarises the way that we all have our own understanding of events, behaviour and information that is derived from our own lens through which we see the world. So when we experience stereotypes that perhaps seem unreasonable, it is important to remember that people construct their own theories based on the information that they have received – which could be the newspaper that they read, which issues information as 'truth', or the experiences they have undergone, which could be those of a child of a parent who was alive during World War Two and who therefore has a particular view of those nations in combat during the war, or who was affected by terrorism.

So stereotypes in themselves cannot be wrong, as we all do it in order to categorise our worlds, but they may not reflect a wider picture and reflective practice helps to bring objectivity to one's own personal construct.

Activity

Challenging stereotypes

Look at this list of people who are often on the receiving end of negative assumptions:

Single parents
Asylum seekers
Only children
Full-time working parents when their child is under six months old
People on benefits
Travellers

> Write down what your first thoughts are – are you using your own perceptions, gathered from your own experience, your family's views, your friend's view, the views of the newspaper you read? Are there any views that you have that might not stand up to close examination? Reflect on your thoughts and make a plan of what you would need to find out that would widen your personal construct.

We should never stop reflecting on how we interact with people. Using the Johari Window (see Table 3.1) can be a way to raise self-awareness.

The Johari Window is a useful model to consider the ways that, in human interaction, individuals are selective about what they share with others (hidden), certainly before they are in a trusted relationship. You will see also that we do not always know what others know about us (blind), perhaps that a parent finds us especially warm, or finds us unapproachable. By trying to manage the shape of the windows so that the 'open' area has the largest amount of shared information, then dialogue and trust can be developed. Work on the 'challenging stereotypes' activity with a partner, using the model of Johari's Window to reflect upon what you know, and what you share, about yourself.

Perceptions of partnerships with parents

Throughout this chapter, there has been reference to working with parents and how we can use reflection to develop our own constructs. We should also consider the reality of working with parents, and what we do. In much of the literature, the expression 'partnership with parents' is used. But what do we actually mean by partnership? Historically, the partnership between practitioners and parents was rooted in a deficit model where parents were judged according to their engagement in the setting (Cottle and Alexander, 2013). It is useful to reflect on whether this is still the case or whether partnership working is more balanced and bi-directional.

In the EYFS Statutory Framework (DfE, 2014), the notion of partnership with parents is stated in the opening page of its introduction, where it is stated that: 'The EYFS seeks to provide partnership working between practitioners and with parents and/or carers' (DfE, 2014, p. 5). The role of the key person is a legal requirement of all registered EYFS settings (DfE, 2014, p. 21), so it is clear that a relationship must be built between settings and families, but there is no further guidance on the activation of that relationship within the statutory framework.

There are mixed views about whether the partnership between parents and practitioners is real or illusory and exactly what the purpose is behind the relationship. For many practitioners, the partnership is the opportunity to share decisions and information

Table 3.1 Johari Window

Hidden	*Unknown*
Known to self	Not known to self
Not known to others	Not known to others
Open	*Blind*
Known to self	Not known to self
Known to others	Known to others

Source: based on the Luft and Ingham Johari Window (1955).

between both parties. For others, it has a more functional and bureaucratic purpose and success is seen through the assimilation of the school views and ethics being reflected within families (Cottle and Alexander, 2013). Gasper descibes the process as a possible tool for empowerment of parents but he recognises the 'invisible boundaries' (Gasper, 2014, p. 195) and the illusion of partnership whilst retaining 'the hierarchical position of superiority' (p. 196).

For practitioners, therefore, reflection on the reality and the equality of the relationship with parents is an element of practice that benefits from regular attention: 'Willingness to engage parents and children is not enough on its own and needs constant review to be true partnership' (Gasper, 2014, p. 196).

Next steps...

Reflective practice now has an established role in many professions, and there are a many different theories, models and tools and resources to use. Finding the most suitable resources can give a practitioner a number of different ways of thinking about a problem or an issue at work. Sometimes, however, there is not enough time to search out websites that inform and offer training resources. This website has a number of resources to use: http://reflectivepractice-cpd.wikispaces.com/Home.

As well as using this resource as an individual, it can also be shared and used as CPD in teams, so staff meetings could use a section or link through to the video clips and models. There are links and resources here to suit all levels and the information has been compiled by those working regularly in the field.

Notes

1 Sarah's case study has been adapted from the training resources *Families Going Forward*© CWDC, DfE and Juliet Neill-Hall.

References

Argyris, C. and Schön, D.A. (1974). *Theory in Practice: Increasing Professional Effectiveness*. San Francisco: Jossey-Bass.

Asmussen, K. (2011) *The Evidence-based Parenting Practitioner's Handbook*. Abingdon: Routledge.

Atkins, S. and Murphy, K. (1994) Reflective practice. *Nursing Standard*, 8(39): 49–56.

Children's Workforce Development Council (CWDC) (2010) *Families Going Forward Learner Resources*. Online: http://webarchive.nationalarchives.gov.uk/20120119192332/http://cwdcouncil.org.uk/families-going-forward-learner-resources, written by Juliet Neill-Hall (accessed 14 December 2014).

Cottle, M. and Alexander, E. (2013) Parent partnership and 'quality' early years services: practitioners' perspectives. *European Early Childhood Education Research Journal*, 22(5): 637–659.

Department for Education (DfE) (2014) *Early Years Foundation Stage: Statutory Framework*. London: DfE.

Dewey, J. (1909) *How We Think* (reprinted 2012). Connecticut: Martino Publishing.

Dryden, L., Forbes, R., Mukherji, P. and Pound, L. (2005) *Essential Early Years*. Abingdon: Hodder Arnold.

Epstein, J. (2008) Improving family and community involvement in secondary schools. *Education Digest*, 73(6): 9–12.

Gasper, M. (2014) How policy has impacted on parents. In Z. Kingdon and J. Gourd (eds) *Early Years Policy: The Impact on Practice*. London: Routledge.

Gibbs, G. (1988) *Learning by Doing: A Guide to Teaching and Learning Methods*. Oxford: Further Education Unit.

Johns, C. (1994). Nuances of reflection. *Journal of Clinical Nursing*, 3: 71–75.

Kelly, G. (1955) *A Theory of Personality: The Psychology of Personal Constructs*. New York: W.W. Norton.

Lindon, J. (2010) *Reflective Practice and Early Years Professionalism*. Oxon: Hodder Education.

Luft, J. and Ingham, H. (1955) The Johari Window, a graphic model of interpersonal awareness. *Proceedings of the Western Training Laboratory in Group Development*, Los Angeles: UCLA.

Moon, J. (2003) *Learning Journals and Logs*. Online: www.ucd.ie/t4cms/UCDTLA0035.pdf (accessed 14 December 2014).

Moon, J.A. (2009) The use of graduated scenarios to facilitate the learning of complex and difficult-to-describe concepts. *Art, Design and Communication in Higher Education*, 8(1): 57–70.

National College for Teaching and Leadership (NCTL) (2013) *Teachers' Standards (Early Years) From September 2013*. London: NCTL.

Schön, D. (1983) *The Reflective Practitioner: How Professionals Think in Action*. London: Temple Smith.

Chapter 4

Supporting transitions and home and setting visits

In this chapter, we shall be looking at:

- links to Early Years Teachers' Standards
- the purpose and value of home visits
- safeguarding issues
- parent and practitioner views on home visits
- maximising the value of setting visits: building trust
- barriers to home visits
- preparing for a home visit
- the setting visit.

This chapter has links to the following EYT Standards:

- 2.3 Know and understand attachment theories, their significance and how effectively to promote secure attachments.
- 2.7 Understand the important influence of parents and/or carers, working in partnership with them to support the child's well-being, learning and development.
- 5.1 Have a secure understanding of how a range of factors can inhibit children's learning and development and how best to address these.
- 5.4 Support children through a range of transitions.
- 6.2 Engage effectively with parents and/or carers and other professionals in the ongoing assessment and provision for each child.
- 7.3 Know and understand child protection policies and procedures, recognise when a child is in danger or at risk of abuse and know how to act to protect them.
- 8.3 Take a lead in establishing a culture of cooperative working between colleagues, parents and/or carers and other professionals.

Introduction

Initial experiences can enhance or taint the process of change, so their management should ensure smooth transitions through phases of the relationship between parents and practitioners and first meetings, where effective use of opportunities can set a seal on future interactions and establish effective, transparent and open communication or negative and defensive blockades. It is helpful to complete training in this area, as the use of strategies to engage parents and encourage trust will help the relationship from the outset. If it is not possible to access suitable training, working with experienced staff will help the preparation.

Transitions

We move through a number of social and cultural transitions throughout life, including events that welcome new babies or rituals that celebrate couple unions, or the arrival of puberty. There are also developmental transitions: from crawling to walking; milk feeding to solids; the hormonal changes which relate to the change from child to adolescent, to the gender-specific changes brought about by the menopause. For young children, the impact of change can be significant, in particular when a parent returns to work and the child moves, for the first time, into provision for education and care.

The transition could be from one setting to another, or from home to setting. It is important to be in regular contact with parents in order to manage these stages effectively as a partnership. Kagan and Neumann talk about vertical and horizontal transitions (Kagan and Neumann, 1998, cited in Vogler *et al.*, 2008, p. 10) in order to distinguish between different types of change:

- Vertical transitions could be from home to setting, or from setting to reception class.
- Horizontal transitions could also be described as 'border crossings' within the various spheres of a child's life, e.g. home to school, school to childminder.
- There may be requirements for the child to adapt their identity (role, dress, behaviour) as they move from one domain to another, which is why it is important for there to be strong cooperation between the domains.

Impact on children

Bulkeley and Fabian (2006) note that the possible effects of transitions on a child can include disaffection, inhibition, behavioural problems and loss of motivation, so planned strategies and effective and overt preparation should be taken to support transitions.

So, in order to support transitions, these are some of the strategies that Bulkeley and Fabian (2006) suggest:

- partnership
- use of play
- social and emotional well-being, which can provide a starting point from which children can explore
- buddy systems and continuity of friendship groups
- building a picture of the transition for children and parents alike.

Fisher (2009) noted that feelings about transition were affected by gender, with boys being more anxious about the transition to year 1, and more boys' parents expressing negative comments about experiences of transition.

Activity

Consider the transition events that take place in your setting – for example, moves into the setting; between rooms; out of the setting. Now consider each of the transitions from the different perspectives of the participants. What are the considerations likely to be? How can the needs of all those involved be met through planning for these transitions?

Transition events can be prepared for through preparatory visits, either from setting to home or from home to setting.

Purpose and value of home visits

The home visit is not a new phenomenon; in fact, the inner London nursery pioneer Margaret MacMillan carried them out in the first part of the twentieth century (Greenfield, 2012). It provides an opportunity for parents to ask questions and practitioners to introduce themselves to the child and family before the settling-in period at the setting. Anecdotally, and supported by Greenfield (2012), the training for this sensitive and fundamentally important role is limited. Greenfield notes that:

> My own experience as a health visitor included academic study, and then visits with experienced colleagues to homes and families from diverse backgrounds and cultures, before I was expected to organise and make visits myself. My first solo visit was still a daunting prospect, as it was hard to predict the type of reception that would be given to a total stranger who hoped to be invited into the home.
>
> (Greenfield, 2012, p. 101)

The purpose of the home visit is 'to allow parents and teachers and practitioners to get to know each other in familiar surroundings, whilst providing children with an opportunity to meet their teacher or key person' (Greenfield, 2012, p. 102), in line with the theory of Bronfenbrenner (2005), which recognises the importance of the cultural context of the child in terms of their development and learning. Practitioners who visit the child at home will have a broader understanding of the experiences that the child has at home, the interests and pre-occupations of the family, the cultural or societal expectations of the family, all of which will have a profound impact on the child.

However, there must be a process in place to ensure that the information is used effectively:

> Practitioners need time to reflect on their visits so that the information can be assimilated. They also need time to share important facts with other nursery workers. The reason for the visit could be lost if teachers are unable to make use of the information. Three teachers explained that time had been spent collecting information that was never used and was locked away and forgotten soon after being given. One teacher in the study described 'feeling a bit like a door to door salesman' when she first started visiting, going from house to house collecting information on a questionnaire in very little time. If she felt this way it is hardly surprising that some parents have similar views.
>
> (Greenfield, 2012, p. 109)

Activity

Uri Bronfenbrenner was the co-founder of the Head Start Programme in the USA.

'Head Start is a federal program that promotes the school readiness of children ages birth to 5 from low-income families by enhancing their cognitive, social and emotional development' (US Department of Health and Human Services, 2014). Bronfenbrenner was also a developmental psychologist who spent much of his professional life with a focus on the influences on children's learning and development. From his studies, he developed the ecological systems theory (Bronfenbrenner, 1979), which argues that children's development does not take place in a vacuum, but it is affected by a range of different experiences (see Chapter 2 for further information).

What information might you obtain from a home visit that you would not get from a setting visit? How does this link to Bronfenbrenner's ecological systems theory?

Greenfield (2012) points out that careful planning should precede the visit in order to make it as positive as possible, ensuring that parents are left at the end of the visit with a sense that the setting values their participation and involvement where possible. Training and shadowing of more experienced practitioners are helpful precursors to leading and planning a visit.

Assessments, judgements and safeguarding

It cannot be disputed that a practitioner on a home visit will be making assessments throughout: about the welfare of the child, the well-being of the child and the development of the child. So parents who feel that there is an element of judgement taking place are, in many ways, absolutely right. A visit to a home can immediately ascertain the levels of literacy, social skills and physical development. It will also enable the practitioner to assess the environment in which the child is based, both physical and emotional.

The skill of making an assessment during the home visit is through thorough preparation beforehand, honest reflection afterwards and the avoidance of judgement based on an opinion that may produce inaccurate results. One useful assessment may be to identify any support needs for a family which is functioning below the poverty line (Aldridge *et al.*, 2012) because practitioners may be able to support families to claim extra entitlements and will be aware of the risk factors which could impact children if they are living in poverty. However, the judgement that a family may be in poverty should not in itself be used to make assumptions about the quality of the relationship, or the well-being of the child, but will be relevant when arranging a time for the visit that is convenient for the parent.

So when a parent is reluctant to have a home visit because they feel as though they may be judged, and worse, they are fearful that their child may be taken away, then this is a concern that should be taken seriously, and respected, because it is true. After all, if there was evidence that a child was being maltreated in the home, then there would be a duty upon the practitioner to report their concerns. All practitioners visiting homes should have a sound understanding of child abuse and what actions they might need to take if they have concerns (DfES, 2006).

Activity

Before you complete your next home visit, ask yourself what factors make an impact on your assessment of the home environment:

Clean, untidy or dirty house?
Few toys?
TV on?

Neighbours/friends present?
Large pets that are not contained?
The ways the child is spoken to and treated?
Smoking indoors?

Think about what you are assessing, and whether any of these factors are potentially safe-guarding issues.

Now consider what might have created the situation that you are witnessing, and what else you would need to do in order to satisfy yourself of the safety of a child.

Parents' and practitioners' view on home visits

The findings from my research indicated that only 15 per cent of parents felt as though home visits made parents feel judged, so from these findings alone it seems that there is little stigma attached. A slightly higher percentage of practitioners (22 per cent) thought parents might feel judged, so it may be a useful activity to consider how parents might feel and indeed how you would feel if you had a home visit. Rather than feeling judged, the visit can, as noted in Pen Green practice, ensure that the 'seeds of trust in the worker can be sown' (Myles *et al.*, 2013, p. 59).

Here are some further parent and practitioner views:

> Home visits are more personal and parents/children are more relaxed. Parents are also likely to be given (a) chance to be more open with information regarding their child.
>
> (Parent)

> I like the fact that we had a home visit. It gave me the chance to discuss some private family issues so I felt happy Michael's home background was understood before he started.
>
> (Parent)

> It gave me a chance to discuss some private family issues so I felt happy that my child's background was understood before he started.
>
> It is a very good opportunity to talk ... because it happens in a familiar environment.
>
> (Parent)

> My son's nursery did a home visit – he loved it and I enjoyed the informal visit to our home.
>
> (Parent)

The last quote also recognises the impact of home visits on children as well. The visit from a practitioner or teacher is likely to be memorable and help children to form associations quickly, so aiding transition to a setting where the practitioner is known to the child. The visit gives practitioners a useful hook for subsequent visits too, when they will also be able to remind the child of the visit – for example: 'Hello, Sam, how is your little hamster Jimi today?' or 'Hello Sam, do you remember the game I brought to your house? Look, it's here!' It is clear that this opportunity to share personal information plays a valuable part in the development of the relationship between parent and setting. For the practitioner, too, the opportunity can be valuable, as it:

> offers the chance for a unique insight into the start of a wonderful partnership between nursery and home. A memorable event which can be key to supporting the child.
>
> (Practitioner)

> The value gained from home visiting is immense.
>
> (Practitioner)

> Excellent way to make parent and child feel at ease as they are on their own territory.
>
> (Practitioner)

> They make parents feel included and valued – give parents and children a chance to be seen in own setting and home territory – brilliant for minority groups, e.g. travellers, forces families, etc.
>
> (Practitioner)

Maximising the value of home visits: trust-building

The home visit is an opportunity to build a strong, trusting and equal partnership that can inform and support the partnership for the length of stay of the child at the setting. A sensitive practitioner will be aware that even confident, chatty parents may be feeling anxious. Trust-building through the home visit involves time, organisation, interest and commitment to the family. From this, the family can see that they are valued and that the staff working in the setting actively make an effort to find out more about the family.

Challenges to home visits

However, there are challenges to home visits, for a number of reasons. One of the biggest barriers to home visits is time and staff resources. The challenges of time constraints were aptly summarised by Sue Greenfield (2012) when carrying out her own field research:

> Time, or the lack of it, was an issue raised by seven of the teachers interviewed. Time constraints put a considerable strain on teachers endeavouring to make a relationship with parents and child in as little as 10 minutes, and at most 45 minutes. The visits were described in the following ways: 'emotionally draining', 'tiring', 'emotional energy', 'you come back shattered'. Time constraints can only add to the stress involved.
>
> (p. 109)

On the other hand, the time is often seen as a worthwhile investment because of the rich information that is shared during this visit. Some settings take a week at the beginning of term to visit all the families. This system is useful for term-time operated settings but will have less value for settings where children are starting at different points during the year.

Anxious families will limit information sharing. Information sharing can be more limited if the family feels anxious about the information that they share.

> Some immigrant families with emergent language skills may fear that there is a chance that they are not properly documented to be in the country. This situation is likely to cause fear and anxiety, which lead to a lack of willingness to communicate openly and trustingly.
>
> (Byrd, 2012, p. 51)

In a previous study, Valdés (1996, cited in Byrd, 2012, p. 45) noted:

> Schools expected a 'standard' family, a family whose members were educated, who were familiar with how schools worked and who saw their role as complementing the teacher's in developing children's academic abilities. It did not occur to school personnel that parents might not know the appropriate ways to communicate with the teachers...

Therefore, it can be helpful if practitioners make the initial meeting with families one that focuses on finding out as much as possible about the family as well as the child, taking into account, through careful questioning, what expectations, concerns and questions the family has.

An additional aspect is consideration about *personal safety*. When making home visits, there are a number of precautions that should be taken in order to be assured of the safety of the visiting team. See the checklist later on in this chapter (p. 48).

Officialdom and clipboards: the impression made at the outset will also influence the rest of the visit. 'The arrival of teachers carrying clipboards holding structured questionnaires and wanting to find out information certainly creates an image of officialdom' (Greenfield, 2012, p. 10). Whilst practitioners may need to record some details, this should not be apparent during introductions. An open, warm and communicative approach will break down barriers and enable the transmission of information to take place much more effectively than a more official presence.

So the reverse of this approach might be more helpful: 'It is important for educators to take the initiative in this process by demonstrating concern, respect and value for all types of families' (Bradley and Schalk, 2013, p. 74).

Activity

Working in pairs or small groups, discuss the pros and cons of initial visits taking place in the family home or in the setting. Try to be as objective as possible, ignoring practice in your own setting for the time being, and thinking about the principles and key points. When you have your list, try to overturn one or two of the barriers that you discussed, in order to create more opportunities for communication.

My research found that, whilst approximately half of all settings were using home visits, there was overwhelming support from both parents (90 per cent) and practitioners (93 per cent). So whilst there is strong support for home visits, they are not happening universally.

Preparing for a home visit

You will want to have a checklist of questions possibly in your head (to be written down later) or on a questionnaire if you feel you cannot manage without one. Green-field says (2012, p. 7) that practitioners found it helpful to have a questionnaire as they were quite nervous too and having some questions made the beginning easier – they were questions about the child. However, be careful of taking written notes early on, so that the family does not feel that you are evaluating them. Documents should appear only after everyone feels comfortable and after you have explained the purpose for the note-taking (Byrd, 2012).

The sorts of questions you will want to ask are likely to be based upon:

- children's interests
- children's likes and dislikes
- children's fears (and, later in the conversation, any families worries)
- children's routines, including eating and sleeping habits
- siblings, relatives, language spoken at home, illnesses – indeed anything that the parent feels would be helpful for you to know.

Here are some other factors to consider:

- Whose responsibility is the management of the visit?
- Who will know where you are?
- Who will you meet with? You should ensure all involved are able to meet with you.
- Are translators needed?
- How will you communicate about the visit? By telephone or email?
- How long will you plan the visit for?
- What do you need to take with you?
- What choices do parents have about the visit?
- What do you need to know about the family in advance?
- What do you want to find out about the family on your visit?
- What do you think the family will want to know from you?
- What will you do if the TV is on?
- What will you do if the neighbour is in?

And some ideas to make the visit a success:

- Bring toys for the children that they can take back to the setting when they start.
- Keep the visit to under an hour.
- Accept water, tea or coffee but nothing else.
- Have an agreed policy on the format of the home visit so there is a consistency – for example, an 'All About Me' form.
- Use a translator if necessary and possible.

- If working with a family who have English as an additional language, make sure that you talk to the carer rather than to the translator (Byrd, 2012).
- Give information about expectations of the setting.

Carrying out a home visit

Ensure your own safety through taking the following precautions:

- Try to visit in pairs if possible.
- Agree a password to use in phone calls if you get into difficulties.
- Always tell someone exactly where you will be and log it into any shared calendars you use.
- Agree to notify a colleague when you have finished the visit, especially if it is the last one of the day.

Activity

Discuss:

What do you want to find out on the visit (to home or to setting)?
How will you record the information you gather?
What do you want the family to find out about you, and the setting?
How will they take this information away with them?

Setting visits

Most settings have a policy on setting visits. You might want to have this document to hand whilst looking at this section. Setting visits will be common for practitioners but they will not be common for the parents, so have a good understanding of how the parent might be feeling, especially if it is their first child and first visit.

Whether the initial visit is a home or setting visit, it is helpful to establish a clear purpose for the meeting (Byrd, 2012), which in this case would be the child settling quickly into a new setting and to bring resources linked to this purpose (such as a news-letter, calendar dates, parents' evenings).

The parent may be:

- excited about returning to work
- dreading the separation
- worried about the costs of childcare
- concerned about the reaction of their child to the setting
- weighing you up
- nervous about talking to you
- upset and anxious.

Setting visits in reception classes are likely to take place with a group of children and so you may not talk to parents on a one-to-one basis. As a lead in the reception class, con-sider whether the parents have the opportunity to talk to you if they have questions that concern them. Is it possible to give each parent five minutes? Whilst you may want to leave them paper and pen to jot down any questions that they may have, those whose literacy is not strong are less likely to reveal their own perceived shortfalls at their child's school, and therefore an opportunity to support and also to understand why the parents may not be helping at home will be lost.

Wherever possible, give parents the opportunity to talk to you in private or to contact you afterwards if there are questions that need to be answered. Many settings use a form for parents to complete which is called 'All about me' or something similar. It is used to find out as much as possible about children before they start in the setting. However, the form's value is that the information is shared with the setting and a good way of building a relationship is to show that you have read this by the time you meet parents.

Alternatives to home

Sometimes a parent will not want a visit in their home, but would be prepared to meet elsewhere. This opportunity could be a positive way to demonstrate the value that you consider the meeting to be, and it will demonstrate its importance to parents. It may be possible to agree to meet in another location, such as a local community centre that the family knows and feels comfortable in.

After the visit

There will be documentation to complete, information to share and a letter to be sent to the family. Follow up on anything agreed at the meeting to demonstrate reliability, consistency and the valuing of this information.

Working with other practitioners during transition

Transition events may be located within a setting or may extend beyond the setting, as in the move to another provider. This will involve working with other professionals, all of whom will bring diverse dimensions in terms of language, values and practice to a multi-professional team.

There has been a consistent move in favour of 'joined up' working as a means of reducing opportunities for children's needs to become lost within work cultures which do not communicate systematically with other agencies. Gasper notes that this change 'has made a significant improvement for those parents and children involved and has enabled better prioritisation of need and more effective targeting of resources (Gasper, 2014, p. 201). However, he notes that change takes time and that there are no 'magic wands or quick fixes' (Gasper, 2014, p. 206).

The current culture in the Children's Workforce, embedded within the legislation enacted in the past two decades and beyond (see Chapter 2), has been to develop joined-up working in order to support families and protect children. Children's Centres in particular have been able to create hubs of information and resources where parents are able to share, learn and receive information. However, there are still barriers to effective communication between different groups of professionals, and this can hamper effective and streamlined support to parents.

> **Activity**
>
> Consider the ways in which you work with other professionals during transitional events. Reflect upon the opportunities that you have to share your practice and knowledge of children, then consider the barriers to effective multi-agency working during phases of transition for children. How can you overcome the barriers that you encounter?

Summary

First meetings with parents and children are significant events, with considerable amounts of information to assimilate, for all parties. The value of listening attentively cannot be over-stated. Take time clarifying points that you are not clear about, showing that you really want to understand more about this family. Listen to what they say about their child, and listen to the child and the ways they interact. It will also help the family if they feel you will understand their feelings, so listening to them will help them feel that you empathise with them, whether their concern is about going back to work and leaving a young child, or helping their child to make friends. Take their concerns seriously, respecting them and asking how they would like you to manage situations (for example, the separation time). If parental fears are dismissed, the relationship will take longer to develop.

> **Next steps...**
>
> Situated within the National Children's Bureau, the PEAL project (NCB, 2007), standing for Parents, Early Years and Learning, has developed a range of training for early years practitioners. It is targeted at all types of early years settings and can be accessed through their website: www.earlychildhood.org.uk/. It is also possible to gain accreditation for parts of the training through the City & Guilds awarding body (part of the Level 3 Work with Parents Award, 3599).

References

Aldridge, H., Kenway, P., MacInnes, T. and Parekh, A. (2012) *Monitoring Poverty and Social Exclusion 2012*. York: Joseph Rowntree Foundation. Online: www.jrf.org.uk/sites/files/jrf/poverty-exclusion-government-policy-summary.pdf (accessed 5 December 2014).

Bradley, J.F. and Schalk, D. (2013) 'Greater than great'. A teacher's home visit changes a young child's life. *Young Children*, July: 70–75.

Bronfenbrenner, U. (1979) *The Ecology of Human Development: Experiments by Nature and Design*. Cambridge, MA: Harvard University Press.

Bronfenbrenner, U. (2005) *Making Human Beings Human: Bioecological Perspectives on Human Development*. London: Sage Publications.

Bulkeley, J. and Fabian, H. (2006) Well-being and belonging during educational transitions. *International Journal of Transitions in Childhood*, 2: 18–31.

Byrd, D.R. (2012) Conducting successful home visits in multicultural communities. *Journal of Curriculum and Instruction*, 6(1): 43–54.

Department for Education and Skills (DfES) (2006) *What to Do If You're Worried a Child Is Being Abused*. Nottingham: DfES.

Fisher, J.A. (2009) 'We used to play in Foundation, it was more funner': investigating feelings about transition from Foundation Stage to year 1. *Early Years*, 29(2): 131–145.

Gasper, M. (2014) How policy has impacted on parents. In Z. Kingdon and J. Gourd (eds) *Early Years Policy: The Impact on Practice*. Abingdon: David Fulton.

Greenfield, S. (2012) Nursery home visits: rhetoric and realities. *Journal of Early Childhood Research*, 10(1): 100–112.

Myles, M., Kiff, L. and Clark, K. (2013) Home visiting from an education and care perspective: getting to know, supporting and working in partnership with parents. In M. Whalley, C. Arnold and R. Orr (eds) *Working with Families in Children's Centres and Early Years Settings*. London: Hodder Stoughton.

National Children's Bureau (NCB) (2007) *Welcome to PEAL*. Online: www.peal.org.uk (accessed 18 August 2014).

US Department of Health and Human Services and Administration for Children and Families (2014) *Office of Head Start*. Online: www.acf.hhs.gov/programs/ohs/about/head-start (accessed 30 July 2014).

Valdés, G. (1996) *Con Respeto: Bridging the Distances Between Culturally Diverse Families and Schools*. New York: Teachers College Press.

Vogler, P., Crivello, G. and Woodhead, M. (2008) *Early Childhood Transitions Research: A Review of Concepts, Theory, and Practice. Working Paper No. 48*. The Hague, The Netherlands: Bernard van Leer Foundation.

Chapter 5

Partnership work with different ages

In this chapter, we shall be looking at:

- links to Early Years Teachers' Standards
- partnership with parents of babies
- partnership with parents of toddlers
- partnership with parents of children with disabilities
- partnership with parents of pre-schoolers
- the key person and trust-building.

This chapter has links to the following EYT Standards:

- 2.2 Demonstrate knowledge and understanding of how babies and children learn and develop.
- 2.3 Know and understand attachment theories, their significance and how effectively to promote secure attachments.
- 3.1 Have a secure knowledge of early childhood development and how that leads to successful learning and development at school.
- 3.3 Demonstrate a critical understanding of the EYFS areas of learning and development and engage with the educational continuum of expectations, curricula and teaching of Key Stage 1 and 2.
- 3.4 Demonstrate a clear understanding of systematic synthetic phonics in the teaching of early reading.
- 5.5 Know when a child is in need of additional support and how this can be accessed, working in partnership with parents and/or carers and other professionals.
- 6.2 Engage effectively with parents and/or carers and other professionals in the ongoing assessment and provision for each child.
- 6.3 Give regular feedback to children and parents and/or carers to help children progress towards their goals.

The relationship between parents and practitioners is likely to vary according to the ages, stages and needs of children, so this chapter will explore a range of factors impacting on the experiences of parents. All stages bring with them different demands and rewards, and no experience will be exactly the same for one parent as another, so listening skills are paramount in identifying the unique issues relating to each family.

In this chapter, the focus will be on babies, toddlers, pre-schoolers and children with disabilities.

Working with parents of babies

Starting with the earliest stages, there are unique issues for practitioners working in baby rooms or with infants. For new parents, there are more factors that could make it difficult for parents to manage their role without support, such as relationship adjustments in the wake of new parenthood, sleep deprivation and postnatal depression.

- Building strong relationships in the early years will set the tone for future relationships between parents and practitioners. A positive experience at this point can have a long-term influence throughout the child's education.
- Infants are influenced by the feelings of their caregivers (Stern, 1995); therefore, reducing the anxiety of the parents is more likely to have a corresponding impact on the stress levels of the infant.
- Research indicates that parents with children under the age of two years place more importance (than those with older children) on the term 'trust' (Department for Education, 2014a). The emotions a parent might experience, when leaving infants of this age, require the input of sensitive and skilled practitioners who can build trust through empathy, listening skills and compassionate relationships with parents and who are themselves practising in a setting which is 'emotionally safe' (Taggart, 2014, p. 17).

As discussed in Chapter 1, the attachment relationship and the development of security and trust between the infant and their caregivers are in a formative and sensitive stage. The developing relationship between the parents and their child is significantly influenced by the parents' own experiences and this can lead to a range of challenges for parents, infants and practitioners working with new parents (Slade and Sadler, 2013), especially because, before trust is established, the practitioner will have no knowledge of the experiences of the parent and their emotional state.

Therefore, it can be particularly useful to understand the perspective of the parent at this stage, taking into account that this transition may be the first time that they have left their child with a professional, and possibly even with a relative, before. There may be many changes taking place in the life of the parent. Apart from the momentous changes of becoming a parent, there will be physical factors which have an impact, such as the effects of a difficult birth, tiredness and breastfeeding. Take a look at the case study below and consider how Jody's mother might be feeling. Think, too, about how you might be feeling and whether you would feel any differently if you knew the following information about Sue.

Case study

Jody is a six-month-old girl who has just started full time at the nursery and you are her key person. It is 6.15 and Jody's mum, Sue, has not arrived. Jody is getting tired and irritable, and so are you. She is not the only one who is still here, and you have your hands full keeping the children cheerful. It is the time of day you like least because, really, all the children want is to go home.

At 6.20, Sue arrives. She looks very stressed and, although she is apologetic, there is something strange about her body language. She seems to be covering her arms right across herself – you're sure you've read about that being a sign of not wanting to be open and friendly.

Sue is a new mother, who has just returned to work after six months' maternity leave. She is breastfeeding and feels it is very important to continue this for as long as possible, because she feels it maintains the bond that she has built up with her daughter, Jody. She has spent the past month trying to adjust her feeding patterns so that the return will not be too much of an upheaval. Breastfeeding does mean that only Sue can feed Jody so she is the one who is up at night, and breastfeeding mums know that they often feed more frequently as breastmilk is digested more easily.

This is her first full week back at work, and Sue is very tired because of the change, the night feeds and getting Jody up and out by 7.15 a.m. She is feeling very sad that she has to go back to work, even though she knows she will adjust and the nursery has an outstanding rating from Ofsted. Her body hasn't yet adjusted to the change in the feeding routine so she has to express milk at lunchtime (in the toilet). This means she only gets ten minutes or so to eat and rest. Her milk leaks when she is full and she is scared that she'll get mastitis. She is very self-conscious about her leaking breasts, exhausted through commuting and feeling guilty because a train derailment means she is late in the first week to pick up Jody. She has tried to ring her partner, Jamie, but he is in a meeting and can't get away before her, even though he works nearer to the nursery. She has tried to ring the nursery but it goes straight to voicemail.

Think about how you respond to parents when they arrive late. Is there anything you do that helps them to trust you and explain more about how they are feeling? Is there anything you feel you might do differently if you had more information?

Beyond the impact of the birth

There may also be psychological factors impacting on the parents, perhaps relating to uncertainty about the best way to bring up children in the light of conflicting advice being received, making decisions about breast or bottle feeding when returning to work, guilt about returning to work or worries about finance. There are many opportunities for parents to obtain advice, but there can be conflicting views when this is sought.

A survey carried out by the National Childbirth Trust, to capture the feelings of women returning to work after maternity leave, found that the most common concern (at 60 per cent) was that of childcare (National Childbirth Trust, 2009). In third and fourth places were concerns about missing their child (56 per cent) and their child missing them (53 per cent), and in fifth place (47 per cent) was the concern of being a good mother. The results of this survey indicate that many mothers return to work with ambivalent feelings about their ability to dovetail working and parenting, and the impact it might have on their child. These concerns may be reduced and accommodated once the initial anxiety of returning to work has faded, but for new parents, these worries may have a significant impact on the relationship that the parent builds with the practitioners in the setting, and it also indicates the value of listening, understanding and supporting new parents through these complex and sometimes overwhelming emotions.

Activity

Since there is no typical parent, there may be some who experience emotions as described above, and others who do not. There may also be a range of different ways that parents express or repress their anxieties about returning to work. Think about the range of reactions that you might meet, and how you might support parents, even when they do not overtly express any anxieties.

Postnatal depression

Amongst the parents returning to work, there will be some women who experience postnatal depression (PND), as it can affect 10 per cent of women in the weeks after the delivery of a new baby, with 'episodes lasting two to six months' (Cooper and Murray, 1998, p. 1885). Other research has also established that PND can arise at any time throughout the year following childbirth (Davies *et al.*, 2003). PND is 'commonly missed by primary care teams' (Cooper and Murray, 1998, p. 1884) and it can have longer term effects on both the mother and the infant, which might include attachment issues and other developmental issues (Stein *et al.*, 2008). Cooper and Murray's review (1998) indicated that support and counselling, through trained health professionals, could alleviate the severity of the PND. It noted that it was not difficult to detect through the use of screening questionnaires, such as the Edinburgh Postnatal Depression Scale, which is used widely and is viewed as a robust tool for the identification of PND (El-Hachem *et al.*, 2014), although it is also observed that detection rates are low, at 46 per cent in one survey (Murray *et al.*, 2004).

Given the rates of occurrence of postnatal depression, the possible causes and the impact on the child may help the partnership relationship in a setting, and since an approximate 35,000 women suffer from this condition untreated every year (4Children, 2011), it is possible that there are families in many settings who are affected. This report re-states the statistics drawn from 1998 research about the mis-diagnosis by primary care health professionals.

Impact on children of postnatal depression

There is also a causal link between poverty and children's outcomes (Field, 2010) and evidence suggests that women with lower socio-economic status are more prone to depression, which may place their children at further risk in terms of their development and learning (Hwa-Froelich *et al.*, 2008; Stein *et al.*, 2008). These factors may all be hidden from the early years practitioner but the potential impact of this information being shared with practitioners by parents is significant and could be far-reaching in terms of provision of support for parent and child. For more information about postnatal depression, see the report 'Suffering in Silence' (4Children, 2011).

Communication

So, it is possible to hypothesise that opportunities to share information and communicate effectively with new parents as they start to leave their children at the nursery may be very important – even more important than previously thought. When looking at my survey, there is a strong focus on communication when filtered for 0–2 years, in responses to a question about the improvement of partnership with parents. The purpose of the key person in settings is exactly that – to improve communication between staff and families. There is a section on the key person towards the end of this chapter.

Working with parents of toddlers

As children grow older and beyond infancy, new developmental stages, achievements and challenges emerge. The toddler years bring with them new phases and opportunities. One commonplace life event for toddlers is the arrival of a new sibling, which requires sensitive interactions and close and strong communication between practitioners and families.

> It's common effective practice to acknowledge when/if a child has a new sibling. The change can cause positive/negative effects on their development/personality, therefore working together with a parent can make home life easier for parent, child and setting.
>
> (Practitioner)

By the time a child is a toddler, the priority in terms of development is likely to be the provision of further social opportunities: learning to play with others and to share and cooperate (DfE, 2012, p. 9), building confidence to develop the child's own interests and to have a positive sense of self (DfE, 2012, p. 11) and considering the feelings of others (DfE, 2012, p. 13).

The relationship will of course still be warm and available, but the practitioner may encourage the child to explore more, to play with others and to develop their own interests. Again, it is important that the family has a strong bond with the practitioner to support activities which might move between the home and the setting (see Chapter 8), such as reading and picture books. It is also an important time in terms of the child's social development, as the outside world will become more familiar and interactions will be taking place at home and in the setting.

At this time, a child's sense of identity and the earliest stages of moral development will be emerging. The development of moral reasoning is associated with (amongst other things) the child's interactions with parents and family (Carlo et al., 2010; Janssens and Deković, 1997; Smetana, 1999). As the child begins to explore boundaries, the close relationship between parent and practitioner can be used to share information in both directions – from parent to practitioners (specific information about the child) and from practitioners to parent (wider information about child development). This relationship can be beneficial to the child as the increased and shared knowledge held by both parent and practitioner can help to maintain stability and consistency for a toddler during a time of change and uncertainty.

What is moral reasoning?

Nucci (1997, p. 128) simply puts it as 'the norms of right and wrong conduct'. Definitions of how people 'ought' to behave, the 'rightness' or 'wrongness' of specific acts, are culturally defined, and contain a number of subjective principles which may vary between societies, even though there is, according to Kohlberg, 'a cultural universality of the sequence of stages' (1981, p. 23). However, regardless of the societal principal, prosocial moral reasoning 'concerns reasoning about conflicts in which the individual must choose between satisfying his or her wants and needs and those of others' (Janssens and Deković, 1997, p. 509).

There is some consensus (Turiel and Rothman, 1972) that the development of moral reasoning is a staged process which moves progressively, but not inevitably, towards higher level reasoning, what Kohlberg (1981) would call the post-conventional level and what Piaget (1948) would call moral relativism. Piaget developed his view of moral reasoning as an extension of his ideas about cognitive development. His model of the stages of moral development (premoral, moral realism and moral relativism) was age related, yet when Kohlberg extended upon Piaget's views and developed another model of moral development, he avoided attaching ages to the stages, which are:

- **Pre-conventional level**
- Stage 1 – avoiding punishment
- Stage 2 – gaining rewards

- **Conventional level**
- Stage 3 – winning approval (good boy)
- Stage 4 – duty, social order

- **Post-conventional level**
- Stage 5 – welfare of community
- Stage 6 – abstract concepts: freedom, justice

(Kohlberg, 1981, pp. 17–18)

There are a number of terms associated with moral reasoning: moral development, empathy (Eisenberg *et al.*, 1991), prosocial behaviour, altruism and theory of mind, for example. In particular, prosocial behaviour is a term that is used more frequently than moral behaviour or prosocial moral behaviour, but it seems that the two are interchangeable (see Keenan and Evans, 2009, p. 307).

The leading cognitive theorists in the field of moral reasoning are Piaget and Kohlberg but, from their starting positions, a number of additional theories have developed. For example, the behaviourist school, with Skinner's theory of operant conditioning playing a significant part, has shown additional dimensions. Skinner's theory was that children are influenced by reinforcers, such as praise and approval, punishment and disapproval. Through the use of these strategies, children can be encouraged to behave in a way that meets the approval of those around them (Keenan and Evans, 2009). In this sense, it can be seen clearly that parents might use reinforcement and praise to encourage their child to adopt an acceptable mode of behaviour, on the basis of what they believe is the morally correct action to take. It is also clear that having a strong rapport and agreed value base with a setting will give children consistent boundaries and agreed expectations. When 'conflicting perspectives are encountered' (Churchill, 2003, p. 114), the child will have to learn that different behaviour is appropriate in different places.

It is very often at this stage of development (between the ages of two and three) that parents may be anxious about their child's behaviour. Children of this age become more aware of the feelings of others, and the EYFS recommends that adults 'set, explain and maintain clear, reasonable and consistent limits so that children can feel safe and secure in their play' (DfE, 2012, p. 13).

Bandura's social learning theory (1977) focuses on the importance of modelling and observational influences that might shape development in behaviours such as 'aggression, helping, sharing' (Keenan and Evans, 2009, p. 30). Those with the opportunity to influence would be the family, parents and siblings during the pre-school years but, once at school, influences may also include teachers, older children and peers (Kochanska et al., 2003). Social learning theory also recognises the significance of the role of the person being observed, in that the behaviour is more likely to be emulated if the person carrying it out behaves sociably and is respected by the observer. For the child whose parents neither behave sociably nor generate respect from the child, a message from another person who may have an influential role on their life may lead to a change in behaviour (BBC Horizon, 2011).

However, whilst a child may develop their understanding of how they ought to behave in a number of ways – through parents, peers or friends (Dunn, 2004; Walker et al., 2000), it is still the parent who has the social role of responsibility for the behaviour of their child. Therefore, building trust with the parent and supporting their parenting needs is an effective way to reduce conduct behaviour problems and maintain value and support for the parent.

Activity

One of the children in your key group has begun to hit and bite other children when asked to share with them. How do you initiate a conversation about this with the parent? What issues might you also be concerned about, having regard to the possibility of the child copying behaviour he has seen? Would any concerns about domestic violence change the way that you approach this situation? In which way/s?

Transition to school

I always think it's nice when parents can walk into the classroom at drop off. Help a child have time to put belongings away. This creates a lot of opportunity to talk.

(Practitioner)

I have accompanied parents on visits to children's next schools. Some parents are nervous about this next step and have told me that to have me there to support them and their child really helped.

(Practitioner)

Helping to relieve anxiety with a child when child settling into new class. Understanding what soothes the child and upsets/scares them.

(Parent)

The phrase 'school readiness' is in current usage and it is used in a variety of ways, with no clear definition. Dame Clare Tickell, in her review of the EYFS (2011) called the term 'ambiguous and emotive' (p. 11), and her approach has been to ensure that children are not 'school unready' as they would be if they were 'not yet toilet trained, able to listen or get on with other children' (Tickell, 2011, p. 20). As a result of this, her recommendations for the Early Years Foundation Stage review (Tickell, 2011) indicated that there should be three areas of fundamental importance for school readiness:

personal, social and emotional development; communication and language; and physical development, which 'are the essential foundations for healthy development, for positive attitudes to relationships and learning, and for progress in key skills such as reading and writing' (Tickell, 2011, p. 20).

The Field Report on the Foundation Years (2010) also mentions school readiness, and again it is not clearly defined, but it can be construed as a preparation for learning efficiently and effectively upon reaching primary school because Field notes that 'greater equality of school readiness would make teaching, particularly in the first few years of primary school, easier and more productive' (p. 42). Field's position appears to be that school readiness can be achieved for the under-fives through equal access to high-quality childcare in order to maximise development and learning before school. The purpose of this is to reduce inequalities caused by poverty:

> By school age, there are very wide variations in children's abilities and the evidence is clear that children from poorer backgrounds do worse cognitively and behaviourally than those from more affluent homes. Schools do not close that gap; children who arrive in the bottom range of ability tend to stay there.
>
> (Field, 2010, p. 5)

Graham Allen's report on the importance of early intervention also considers school readiness (2011), but focuses more on social and emotional competences with which to manage school attainments: 'Only by ensuring that children have this basic foundation of social and emotional skills will we be able to ensure that they are school ready, life ready and child ready' (Allen, 2011, p. 8). The issue of literacy has taken centre stage in the debate on school readiness, and methods of learning to read have been contested and are still lacking a consensus. Parents may value some clarification on the use of phonics to support reading and how prepared their child should be. The EYFS Early Learning Goal for *Literacy: Reading* requires that:

> Children read and understand simple sentences. They use phonic knowledge to decode regular words and read them aloud accurately. They also read some common irregular words. They demonstrate understanding when talking with others about what they have read.
>
> (DfE, 2012, p. 29)

The EYFS Early Learning Goal for *Literacy: Writing* requires that:

> Children use their phonic knowledge to write words in ways which match their spoken sounds. They also write some irregular common words. They write simple sentences which can be read by themselves and others. Some words are spelt correctly and others are phonetically plausible.
>
> (DfE, 2012, p. 31)

Early Years Teachers' Standards require those achieving the status to have: 'Standard 3.4: A clear understanding of systematic synthetic phonics in the teaching of early reading' (NCTL, 2013, p. 3). So whilst there are some expectations that 'school-readiness' requires reading and writing, there are others that focus more on the emotional skills required to manage the transition into a new setting. The government's document *Families in the Foundation Years: Evidence Pack* (DfE, 2011) recognises the essential ingredient of early years learning: play, noting that: 'Professionals help children to develop and learn through play' (slide 42). Opportunities for creative play during the early years is a thread that runs through the EYFS and is the framework within which children learn and process their developing skills, whether those are the acquisition of emotional strengths that give them the inner resilience to manage transitions or the practical development of skills for language and literacy.

It is hoped that the transition between EYFS and KS1 manages this important adjustment for children, and that practitioners are able to support parents through this stage, through listening to parents about their own perspectives on school readiness and what that might mean to them too. For parents, for example, their anxiety may be whether they are supporting their children sufficiently so that they will flourish at school and have positive outcomes and life chances. They may alternatively be concerned that their child eats at lunchtime and is able to go to the toilet on their own.

Activity

What do you do to support parents in these three distinct phases of infancy, toddlerhood and pre-school? Is there one area in which you are most involved? Which do you think is the most challenging when working with parents and how might you work with colleagues to support families?

Talk to colleagues about the commonalities and distinctions between these age groups and the needs of parents in terms of information and support. Consider your current provision and identify ways to develop your current practice, based on your own reflections.

Consider how you share your knowledge of the value of play with parents in your setting.

Partnership with parents of children with disabilities

Parents care for children with disabilities from infancy to adulthood and often beyond; however, their relationships with professionals are influenced by the additional elements of caring for a disabled child. This can widen the gap between parent and 'expert' and position parents as the ones in need of support and knowledge, rather than both professionals and parents being in need of further information that the other participant has and which is vital (both professional knowledge and individual knowledge of that child) for ongoing diagnosis and management of conditions (Hodge and Runswick-Cole, 2008).

The Children and Families Act 2013 has made a number of significant changes to parental rights within disability support, which have been codified within the new Special Educational Needs Code of Practice (DfE/DoH, 2014): 'There is a clearer focus on the participation of children and young people and parents in decision-making at individual and strategic levels' (p. 14).

Other changes within the SEN Code of Practice mean that:

* the age range of individuals who are supported by the Code has been extended up to the age of 25 years
* there is a new Education, Health and Care plan to replace statements and Learning Difficulty Assessments

- families must be made aware of the Local Offer of support available to them
- there is an expectation that the principle of joint working between education, health and care is implemented effectively
- there is increased family control through personal budgets.

The SEN Code of Practice (DfE/DoH, 2014) also reminds us of the importance of ensuring the safety of disabled children through their link to the 2013 version of 'Working Together to Safeguard Children', as it is known that disabled children are amongst those at greater risk of all types of abuse (NSPCC, 2014).

Disability within a family (whether parent or child) also has an associated link with poverty:

- In 2009/10, families with at least one disabled member were 30 per cent more likely to live in poverty than families without disabilities (Child Poverty Action Group, n.d.).

So parents of disabled children face the initial challenge of the disability but then encounter further challenges which make their role even more difficult and exhausting.

What might parents need?

An understanding of the stresses (as above, likelihood of financial impact and child protection issues) associated with living with a child with a disability is gained through research, training and local knowledge of resources and support opportunities.

Since the implementation of the Children Act of 2004, a culture of information sharing and the maintenance of parental and child involvement within support and caring processes have been a priority. The spirit of the *Every Child Matters* agenda (DfES, 2003) maintains a framework of outcomes, which includes *Being Healthy*, so together with legislative frameworks, parents should have access to effective support and resources. There are a number of reviews of children's development which take place during the first five years (two-year-old check, health visitors' Healthy Child Programme review, EYFS profile). These assessments are all in the process of change, with the two-year-old check and the Healthy Child Programme becoming an integrated review and the EYFS Profile being be replaced by a baseline assessment in schools.

However, new legislation requires time for training and implementation in order to become embedded, and there is considerable research which indicates that parenting a disabled child increases the likelihood of stress-related conditions (including depression) in parents (Hastings and Beck, 2004).

Why might parents of children with special educational needs (SEN) choose a particular setting?

> Over half (52 per cent) of parents of children with a disability said they found it easy to travel to the nearest childcare provider who could accommodate their child's condition. However, fewer parents agreed that there are providers in their area who can cater for their child's condition (39 per cent), that the hours available fitted with their commitments (35 per cent) or that it was easy to find suitable childcare in the area (30 per cent). Of those who used a provider, just over three in

five (61 per cent) said that staff were trained in how to deal with their child's condition.

(Department for Education, 2014a, p. 20)

In the childcare survey, the question was raised of whether the perceptions of suitable childcare that parents held was based on the actual availability or the information available to them about suitable childcare.

Activity

How does your setting support children with special educational needs and disabilities? How do you share this information with parents? Is updated information fed to the Family Information Service? Do you ensure that staff are trained to support disabilities, and know how to access additional support when needed? The new Special Educational Needs Code of Practice was implemented from September 2014. Specific guidance related to the early years has been produced by the Department for Education (DfE, 2014b).

Whilst produced before the new SEN Code of Practice was published, using the audit tool Multi Agency Planning and Improvement Tool (Early Support, 2012) is a useful way of identifying your level of provision and training staff in the delivery of high-level services in this area. See the reference list for the hyperlink.

The key person

For all children who attend settings in their pre-school years, from infants to pre-schoolers, disabled or otherwise, the relationship with a parent who is choosing a setting for their first child will be complemented by the 'settled relationship' with the key person (DfE, 2014c, p. 18). One practitioner describes the benefits:

> Having parent and key person meetings, giving the parents the chance to really get to know the key person, to discuss development and overall build a relationship that can establish trust and belief that the child is safe and will develop with that person.
>
> (Practitioner)

A parent's anxieties should be lessened through the relationships with a skilled key person to build strong relationships with the child and also other family members. Regular and consistent interactions and open communication will strengthen the relationship, although for some harder-to-reach families, reaching the desired point will take time, commitment and patience. The Early Years Foundation Stage gives examples of the ways in which practitioners can build trust with parents:

> At times of transition make sure that staff greet and say goodbye to babies and their carers. This helps to develop secure and trusting three-way relationships.
>
> (Early Education, 2012, p. 8)

> Discover from parents the copying games that their babies enjoy, and use these as the basis for your play.
>
> (Early Education, 2012, p. 8)

It may be a three-way relationship but, for a practitioner, it is helpful to ensure under-standing and knowledge of as many family members as possible, because all family members who are in touch with the child will have an impact on their development (Bronfenbrenner, 1979) and also because this widening of the boundaries of family support can give insights about behaviour, attitudes and assumptions.

The basis of the key person approach is grounded within attachment theory (see Chapter 1), which was introduced by John Bowlby (1953), but it is Peter Elfer's work with his colleagues Elinor Goldschmeid and Dorothy Selleck (Elfer *et al.*, 2003, 2012) that illustrates the practical benefits and challenges of ensuring a strong relationship in a setting with practitioners who are well-known to their key children. Elfer *et al.* (2003, p. 18) note: 'The key person approach is a way for working in nurseries in which the whole focus and organisation is aimed at enabling and supporting close attachments between individual children and individual nursery staff.'

A number of the issues of this dimension of early years work have been explored in recent papers (Page and Elfer, 2013; Taggart, 2011). These challenges not only relate to the well-being of the child and the satisfaction of the relationship for the parent, but also raise evidence that some practitioners 'fear the consequences for themselves, of the repeated painfulness of losses of attachment when children make transitions' (Barnett, 1995, cited in Page and Elfer, 2013). But for all the challenges, the key person is a requirement of the EYFS (DfE, 2014c, p. 18). Elfer *et al.* (2003) argued for key person practice to be implemented in nurseries (the later edition widens this to 'early years') for a number of reasons, involving the benefits of enabling practitioners to be responsive to the needs of the child, to anticipate the distress of an unknown experience and to hold or contain the child, both physically and emotionally. The EYFS endorses this: 'Be close by and available' (DfE, 2012, p. 10). Elfer and colleagues explain that, in pre-language stages, a practitioner who wants to build a relationship with a baby needs to understand what the baby means when he or she is crying, which requires close atten-tion to non-verbal cues and active steps to identify the cause of distress and the possible remedies. The advantage for parents is that it gives them 'the chance to liaise with someone else who is fully committed and familiar with their baby or child' (Elfer *et al.*, 2003, p. 18). For parents, it also means that there is a named person with a deeper understanding of their child, taking responsibility for caregiving functions such as feeding, nappy changing and comforting. For the child, there is a designated person who knows them and who offers emotional support as well as attendance to intimate care, such as nappy changing and toileting.

Activity

The key person is now a requirement for all settings, but the finer details of the role will vary between settings. Reflect upon your practice and how you have maintained a balance in your caring relationships with children and families. Is there a boundary in place in your practice and, if so, was it positioned by you, by your setting or in response to the prefer-ences of the families with whom you work? Consider what you would feel to be over-stepping the boundary and how you would know that had happened? Is this an area of practice that is discussed at all at your setting or in staff training?

Summary

One of the most important aspects of parenting support is to value their contribution to their child's development, and this can be done through listening, responsiveness and open-mindedness.

> Make time to listen to what the parent has to say without being judgemental and without making them feel that they have restricted time.
>
> (Practitioner)

Next steps...

This chapter highlights some of the 'emotional complexity of nursery work' (Dearnley and Elfer, 2007, p. 277), such as the management of one's own feelings, building relationships with children that involve care and emotional investment, yet remain professionally boundaried, and working closely with parents who may feel insecure if their child is perceived to have a strong(er) bond with the practitioner than with them. There is a delicate path to maintain in terms of making professional judgements in relation to safeguarding or onward referral to ensure the safety of the child; respecting and acknowledging the greater knowledge and understanding of the parent in terms of their own child.

The articles by Dearnley and Elfer (2007) and Taggart (2011; 2014) consider the topic of emotional labour in more depth. Consider your own practice and your emotional investment in relation to the children in your care. Reflect on your own experiences in childhood and your experiences of being parented. Consider too the question of how much 'emotional labour' and 'caring' is part of your role and how it affects your professional practice.

Before a staff meeting, provide staff members with links to these articles and encourage them to read at least one of them. Discuss the implications of the 'care' and 'professional' aspects of roles. Share any concerns.

References

4Children (2011) *Suffering in Silence: 70,000 Reasons Why Help With Postnatal Depression Needs to Be Better*. London: 4Children. Online: www.4children.org.uk/Resources/Detail/Suffering-in-Silence (accessed 12 December 2014).

Allen, G. (2011) *Early Intervention: The Next Steps. An Independent Report to Her Majesty's Government*. London: HM Government.

Bandura, A. (1977) *Social Learning Theory*. Englewood Cliffs, NY: Prentice Hall.

BBC Horizon (2011) *Are You Good or Evil?* Online: www.bbc.co.uk/programmes/b014kj65 (first broadcast 7 September 2011).

Bowlby, J. (1953) *Childcare and the Growth of Love*. London: Penguin.

Bronfenbrenner, U. (1979) *The Ecology of Human Development: Experiments by Nature and Design*. Cambridge, MA: Harvard University Press.

Carlo, G., Mestre, M.V., Samper, P., Tur, A. and Armenter, B.E. (2010) The longitudinal relations among dimensions of parenting styles, sympathy, prosocial moral reasoning, and prosocial behaviours. *International Journal of Behavioral Development*, 35: 116–124.

Child Poverty Action Group (n.d.) *Who Lives in Poverty?* Online: www.cpag.org.uk/content/who-lives-poverty (accessed 20 October 2014).

Churchill, S.L. (2003) Goodness-of-fit in early childhood settings. *Early Childhood Education Journal*, 31(2): 113–118.

Cooper, P.J. and Murray, L. (1998) Postnatal depression. *British Medical Journal*, 316: 1884–1886.

Davies, B.R., Howells, S. and Jenkins, M. (2003) Early detection and treatment of postnatal depression in primary care. *Journal of Advanced Nursing*, 44(3): 248–255.

Dearnley, K. and Elfer, P. (2007) Nurseries and emotional well-being: evaluating an emotionally containing model of professional development. *Early Years: An International Journal of Research and Development*, 27(3): 267–279. Online: http://repository.tavistockandportman.ac.uk/95/1/Dearnley_Nurseries.pdf (accessed 25 March 2015).

Department for Education (DfE) (2011) *Families in the Foundation Years: Evidence Pack*. London: DfE.

Department for Education (DfE) (2012) *Development Matters in the Early Years Foundation Stage*. London: DfE/Early Education.

Department for Education (DfE) (2013) *Working Together to Safeguard Children*. London: DfE. Online: www.gov.uk/government/publications/working-together-to-safeguard-children (accessed 19 October 2014).

Department for Education (DfE) (2014a) *Childcare and Early Years Survey of Parents 2012–2013*. Report SFR 06/2014 (Huskinson, Kostadintcehva, Greevy, Salmon, Dobie, Medien, Gilby, Littlewood and D'Souza). London: DfE.

Department for Education (DfE) (2014b) *Early Years: Guide to the 0–25 SEND Code of Practice. Advice for Early Years Providers that Are Funded by the Local Authority*. London: DfE. Online: www.gov.uk/government/uploads/system/uploads/attachment_data/file/350685/Early_Years_Guide_to_SEND_Code_of_Practice_-_02Sept14.pdf (accessed 20 October 2014).

Department for Education (DfE) (2014c) *Statutory Framework for the Early Years Foundation Stage*. London: DfE.

Department for Education and Skills (DfES) (2003) *Every Child Matters: Summary*. London: DfES.

Department for Education/Department of Health (DfE/DoH) (2014) *Special Educational Needs and Disability Code of Practice: 0 to 25 Years*. London: DfE/DoH. Online: www.gov.uk/government/publications/SEND-code-of-practice-0-to-25 (accessed 25 March 2015).

Dunn, J. (2004) *Children's Friendships: The Beginnings of Intimacy*. Oxford: Blackwell.

Early Education (2012) *Development Matters in the Early Years Foundation Stage (EYFS)*. London: Early Education.

Early Support (2012) *Multi Agency Planning and Improvement Tool*. London: DoH. Online: http://councilfordisabledchildren.org.uk/media/537314/mapit_document_april_2013.pdf (accessed 14 December 2014).

Eisenberg, N., Fabes, R.A., Schaller, M., Carlo, G. and Miller, P.A. (1991) The relations of parental characteristics and practices to children's vicarious emotional responding. *Child Development*, 62(6): 1393–1408.

Elfer, P., Goldschmeid, E. and Selleck, D. (2003) *Key Persons in the Nursery: Building Relationships for Quality Provision*. London: David Fulton.

Elfer, P., Goldschmeid, E. and Selleck, D.Y. (2012) *Key Persons in the Early Years*, 2nd edition. Abingdon: Routledge.

El-Hachem, C., Rohayem, J., Khalil, R.B., Richa, S., Kesrouani, A., Gemayel, R., Aouad, N., Hatab, N., Yaghi, N., Salameh, S. and Attieh, E. (2014) Early identification of women at risk of postpartum depression using the Edinburgh Postnatal Depression Scale (EPDS) in a sample of Lebanese women. *BMC Psychiatry*, 14: 242. Online: www.biomedcentral.com/1471-244X/14/242 (accessed 25 March 2015).

Field, F. (2010) *The Foundation Years: Preventing Poor Children Becoming Poor Adults: The Report of the Independent Review on Poverty and Life Chances*. London: HM Government.

Hastings, R.P. and Beck, A. (2004) Practitioner review: stress intervention for parents of children with intellectual difficulties. *Journal of Child Psychology and Psychiatry*, 45(8): 1338–1349.

Hodge, N. and Runswick-Cole, K. (2008) Problematising parent–professional partnerships in education. *Disability & Society*, 23(6): 637–647.

Hwa-Froelich, D.A., Loveland Cook, C.A. and Flick, L.H. (2008) Maternal sensitivity and communication styles. *Journal of Early Intervention*, 31(1): 44–66.

Janssens, J.M.A.M. and Deković, M. (1997) Child rearing, prosocial moral reasoning and prosocial behaviour. *International Journal of Behavioral Development*, 20(3): 509–527.

Keenan, T. and Evans, S. (2009) *An Introduction to Child Development*. London: Sage.

Kochanska, G., Aksan, N. and Nichols, K.E. (2003) Maternal power assertion in discipline and moral discourse contexts: commonalities, differences, and implications for children's moral conduct and cognition. *Developmental Psychology*, 39: 949–963.

Kohlberg, L. (1981) *Essays on Moral Development Volume 1: The Philosophy of Moral Development*. San Francisco: Harper and Row.

Murray, L., Woolgar, M. and Cooper, P. (2004) Detection and treatment of postpartum depression. *Community Practitioner*, 77(1): 13–17.

National Childbirth Trust NCT (2009) *The Experiences of Women Returning to Work After Maternity Leave in the UK. A Summary of Survey Results*. London: NCT. Online: www.nct.org.uk/parenting/returning-work-after-maternity-leave (accessed 18 October 2014).

National College for Teaching and Leadership (NCTL) (2013) *Teachers' Standards (Early Years) From September 2013*. London: NCTL.

National Society for Prevention of Cruelty to Children (NSPCC) (2014) *'We Have the Right to Be Safe'. Protecting Disabled Children from Abuse*. London: NSPCC. Online: www.nspcc.org.uk/preventing-abuse/research-and-resources/right-to-be-safe (accessed 13 December 2014).

Nucci, L. (1997) Moral development and character formation. In H.J. Walberg and G.D. Haertel (eds) *Psychology and Educational Practice*. Berkeley: MacCarchan.

Page, J. and Elfer, P. (2013) The emotional complexity of attachment interactions in nursery. *European Early Childhood Education Research Journal*, 21(4): 553–567.

Piaget, J. (1948) *The Moral Judgment of the Child*. New York: Free Press.

Slade, A. and Sadler, L.S. (2013) Minding the baby: complex trauma and home visiting. *International Journal of Birth and Parenting Education*, 1: 50–53.

Smetana, J.G. (1999) The role of parents in moral development: a social domain analysis. *Journal of Moral Education*, 28(3): 311–321.

Stein, A., Malmberg, L.-E., Sylva, K., Barnes, J., Leach, P. and the Families, Children and Child Care project team (2008) The influence of maternal depression, caregiving and socioeconomic status in the postnatal year on children's language development. *Child: Care, Health and Development*, 34(5): 603–612.

Stern, D. (1995) *The Motherhood Constellation*. London: Karnac Books.

Taggart, G. (2011) Don't we care? The ethics and emotional labour of early years professionalism. *Early Years*, 31(1): 85–95.

Taggart, G. (2014) Compassionate pedagogy: the ethics of care in early childhood professionalism. *European Early Childhood Education Research Journal*, online 29 October 2014. doi: 10.1080/1350293X.2014.970847.

Tickell, C. (2011) *The Early Years: Foundations for Life, Health and Learning*. London: Department for Education.

Turiel, E. and Rothman, G.R. (1972) The influence of reasoning on behavioral choices at different stages of moral development. *Child Development*, 43(3): 741–756.

Walker, L.J., Hennig, K.H. and Krettenauer, T. (2000) Parent and peer contexts for children's moral reasoning development. *Child Development*, 71(4): 1033–1048.

Chapter 6

Parent-friendly environments

In this chapter, we shall be looking at:

- links to Early Years Teachers' Standards
- creating an inclusive environment for all parents
- strengths-based practice
- the partnership model of working with parents
- practitioners' and parents' views on creating a parent-friendly environment.

A parent-friendly setting links to the following EYT Standards:

- 5.3 Demonstrate a clear understanding of the needs of all children, including those with special educational needs and disabilities, and be able to use and evaluate distinctive approaches to engage and support them.
- 8.1 Promote equality of opportunity and anti-discriminatory practice.

The environment in an early years setting can encourage or inhibit parents, carers or families and also children from becoming more engaged with a setting, making it a powerful and effective opportunity that practitioners who are working with parents should reflect upon and review on a regular basis.

Activity

Think about an unfamiliar environment that you have visited in the last year. It could be somewhere official, or a visit to someone's home. How did you feel as you arrived? What was it that made you feel comfortable and at ease when you arrived (or not)?

What did you see? Think? Feel? Smell? Share your thoughts with a partner and then work together to summarise what stimulated your feelings. These points may trigger thoughts:

> This element of the environment...
> ...made me feel that I belong here.
> ...made me feel that the people here were warm and friendly.
> ...helped me to get the correct information.
> ...made me feel that people are interested in my welfare.
> ...encouraged me to trust the people there.
> ...gave me a sense that the place was well organised.

Parents' feedback to the question 'What makes a setting feel parent-friendly'?

'A smiling face!'
'Approachable staff.'
'Being greeted when you arrive.'
'Friendly, open people.'
'Information displayed for parents.'
'Making parents feel at ease.'
'Open doors, welcoming teachers who are approachable and effective.'

Practitioners who want to create a parent-friendly environment may spend a great deal of time reflecting, adjusting, tweaking, adding more adjustment and listening and observing the parents who visit the setting in an effort to make them feel comfortable there, because the evidence is clear, from a range of sources, that it is important to work together with parents (Department for Education and Skills, 2007).

However, this work can be challenging for a number of reasons.

• Parents may not feel confident to engage with the setting.
• Parents may be too busy to engage at times when the setting is open.
• There may be resistance to change from colleagues.
• It will take time to build links with all parents.

A sense of optimism that you do have the capacity to change entrenched beliefs from both parents and colleagues for the benefit of the children in the setting is likely to have a contagious effect. The rationale for this involvement remains the same: that children whose parents are involved and interested in their learning are at a greater advantage in terms of achievement and outcomes than those whose parents are not, and this can be of particular importance for poorer children whose risk factors for disadvantage are higher than those who are not poor and whose parental involvement is a strong factor to improve their life chances (Blanden, 2006; Field, 2010).

This practitioner talks in terms of the 'unit' of parent and child and the importance of treating them holistically:

> I've been thinking about parents and parent partnership … most of the time my focus is well and truly on the child, but it's interesting to really think about the parents and this makes me think about the unit – at the heart of meeting with the parents, generally, the focus will be the child. But if we focus on what support a parent might need so they can sort that out, then the unit will be healthier and so the child will be healthier.

An inclusive environment for all parents

The purpose of maintaining a parent-friendly environment is to encourage engagement with parents so that they have a sense of belonging to the setting, an element of ownership. However, as Nutbrown and Clough rightly point out, 'Inclusion must not be imposed from without, but developed in partnership with those who seek it' (2013,

p. 4). It is not for the practitioners to decide how groups should be included, but to engage with and listen to parents and carers in order to understand their needs. Many settings welcome predominantly mothers, though there are increasing numbers of fathers who share the responsibilities of childcare (Fatherhood Institute, 2011), and some families may also use extended members of the family, such as grandparents and step-parents, to visit the setting. The question of who may constitute a family member is also part of the more complex family arrangements that are now a part of the lives of many children, and an inclusive environment will take into account the diversity and wealth of ages, orientations and heritages who will be working with you in partnership. This includes:

- mothers and fathers of all ages
- same-sex parents
- grandparents
- foster carers
- adoptive parents
- parents whose first language is not English
- parents who have a range of cultural and religious values
- childminders and nannies
- step-parents and other extended family members.

The list crosses gender, age, heritage and cultural boundaries and working with them are groups of practitioners and key people whose aim is to help the child to progress. Their commitment and engagement in the process of drawing parents and carers into the creation of a children's world which spans home and setting is one simple key to the development of a community around the child. It is easy to put up posters with greetings in a number of different languages, or show images of fathers involved with their children, or playing a non-traditional role in some way. Whilst this might get parents through the doors, only a strong relationship within the setting, through the genuine interest and commitment of the practitioners and parents, will maintain the partnership. It is not difficult to demonstrate aspects of partnership with parents, but it is harder to work beyond a superficial level and it takes constant reflection and revision of practice.

Iram Siraj-Blatchford indicates that there are many opportunities to develop further in relation to the inclusion of all families:

> While most early childhood settings appear to be calm and friendly places on the surface, I argue that there may be a great deal of underlying inequality. This may appear through the implementation of differential policies, adult interactions, the use of displays, or through variations (or lack of variation) in the planning, curriculum or programme that the staff offer to individuals or groups.
>
> (Siraj-Blatchford, 2014, p. 182)

This is a challenging statement, but one for reflection.

Activity

Think about one aspect from the quote above: adult interactions. How do you interact with the adults who come into the setting? Is there any common practice that you use? Are there some adults with whom you feel more comfortable talking? Explore what it is that makes it easier. Then think about adults that you find it difficult to interact with. Can you identify any barriers? Once you have done that, consider what steps have already been taken in the setting to improve practice. How can you progress from here?

Whatever the situation, it can be difficult to form positive relationships with parents who do not seem motivated to become involved in their children's learning. It is also difficult for practitioners to admit that they dread the appearance of a parent who is regularly aggressive, or seems to be disinterested in their child. This is not uncommon though; the issue is more that it is hard to admit it.

Nutbrown and Clough (2013) used interview transcripts to demonstrate the complexity of the challenge for practitioners who were reluctant to admit (while recording) their agreement with one person who has spoken of her dislike of one of the parents.

> Later we realised that Mandy had put into words the feelings of some other participants in the group. They too sometimes resented those parents who seemed neglectful and they thought (not without guilt) that they treated such parents differently – perhaps making less effort to include them or have conversations with them about their children.
>
> (p. 125)

These practitioners did not make these statements lightly. It is unlikely that any of them would argue against the principles of equal treatment for all parents, which explains the guilt that they experienced. But we cannot like all parents. It is forgivable to find some parents irritating, or selfish, especially when one has a strong professional ethic which means that the child has primacy and their development is the priority. But it is this very professionalism that can be tapped into to review practice and to build relationships with all parents, whatever the personal feelings may be. The investment of time and patience will be needed, and it will not always make any difference at all, but it will show how much can be achieved in order to engage parents and learn from them.

One practitioner had this to say about building bonds with parents when it is not easy:

> Tenacity: keeping on, keeping on, keeping on. Slowly, slowly, drip, drip, drip. Sometimes there are an awful lot of barriers. My way of understanding is that part of the work with the child is the work with the parent. A parent may be very mistrusting, with cultural differences, language barriers, being fairly new to the country, so the more work you can do to build trust, that has an impact on a parent which has a knock on impact with the child and family that maybe people can be trusted. You've got to build that trust at a pace that is tolerable to parents.
>
> If you personally find something difficult on a subjective level, you have to try to leave your own feelings outside the door and try to understand the parent, and it might be quite difficult for you to understand if they are aggressive or offensive. But there's a much better chance of building bridges if you can leave your own feelings behind, which might help to understand their feelings. The barrier might be with you.

Welcoming and involving all parents

We know that there is no such thing as a typical parent. Parents are male, female, lesbian, homosexual, heterosexual, old, young, in partnership, divorced, lone, rich, poor and from a range of different religious and cultural heritages. All of these factors can have an impact on social norms, expectations and behaviour, so settings must find a way to ensure that all members of this richly diverse group find a welcome and a sense of belonging in the setting. Key points from one or two groups are explored here.

Gender

Most settings are populated and staffed overwhelmingly by women, putting men in a position of the 'other' in the setting. But there are far more men taking their children to school and nursery now than at any time in the past, and settings are taking that into account through the use of dad's days and 'adapting our approach to attract the fathers' (Whalley et al., 2013, p. 157).

A willingness to build the relationship with fathers as well as mothers can be more difficult than anticipated, and some practitioners do find this difficult, because they are so used to relating to mothers. However, there is consistent evidence which shows the benefits for children of fathers' involvement, which includes: 'better peer relationships; fewer behaviour problems; lower criminality and substance abuse; higher educational/occupational mobility relative to parents' employment; capacity for empathy; non-traditional attitudes to earning and childcare; more satisfying adult sexual partnerships; and higher self-esteem and life-satisfaction' (Burgess, n.d., p. 29). But, in recent research about children's service practitioners working with fathers, it was noted that:

> Having male staff was not noted as important. This may reflect the reality that having a same-gender worker is much less important than the interpersonal skills of a worker of whatever sex. However, it may also reflect the reality that male staff members are simply not available in most family services.
>
> (Scourfield et al., 2014, p. 8)

So there are ways to emphasise to fathers that they are part of the parenting dynamic. For example:

* use 'Dear Mums and Dads' rather than 'Dear Parents'
* ensure that documentation includes both parents and their status
* ask parents how they would like to be engaged in the setting.

But it is also about the relationship with fathers. Some settings:

* train staff to communicate with men as well as women
* gather information from all parents about the types of activities they would value
* find out more about the interests of all parents in order to develop conversations and build trust.

Working with separated couples

The nature of a relationship breakdown will have an impact on the way a setting is able to engage with a couple who have separated. It can help the family if the setting can take a child-centred approach and maintain parents' focus on the importance of the welfare of the child. The amount of time that a father spends with his children will be affected by a number of factors, 'including his satisfaction with his employment, his relationship with his own father, his mental well-being and his attitudes towards parenting' (Belsky, 1984 and Pleck, 2007, cited in Asmussen and Weizel, 2009). But the authors of the review 'Engaging and working with parents' (Asmussen and Weizel, 2009) note also that: 'The quality of a father's relationship with his children's mother is perhaps the strongest predictor of the quality and time he spends with his children' (p. 6).

This indicates that the mother is often the gatekeeper to access to the children. There may, therefore, be opportunities to highlight to parents the benefits of parental engagement from the perspective of the child. Whalley et al. (2013) presented a case study of a practitioner who worked with both parents who were locked in adversity, by staying mindful of the needs of the child to have access to both parents, in a positive relationship. By avoiding becoming involved but supporting both parents without bias, the child's needs were met.

Lesbian and gay parents

Whether or not there are children with gay or lesbian parents in your setting, you are likely to know that children's well-being will not be affected through living with same-sex parents in itself (Guasp, 2010), but there may be more impact on a child as a result of the reactions of others – for example, if other parents discourage their own child's friendship or limit visits to the home.

In her research, April Guasp (2010) interviewed the children of lesbian and gay parents and noted:

> Children want to see gay people and their families talked about and celebrated in primary school. This would mean that all children learn about gay people in a positive way, not just from negative comments, and it would mean that children with gay parents could stop being the people who have to educate everyone else.
>
> (Guasp, 2010, p. 28)

Whilst legislation prevents discrimination against lesbian and gay parents, attitudes take time to change and this can sometimes be explained by a lack of information and a fear of 'otherness' (Holmström, 2013). However, as far as the children are concerned, their family is the same as any other. Here are some of the key findings from the research:

> Many children of gay parents see their families as special and different because all families are special and different, though some feel that their families are a lot closer than other people's families. Some children feel that their family is a bit different if they have lesbian or gay parents but this is something to celebrate, not worry about. Other children do recognise that children with gay parents are less common than other sorts of families, but don't feel this means that their families are any different

to other people's families because of it. Very young children don't think their families are different from other people's families at all.

(Guasp, 2010, p. 3)

The main issue for children of lesbian and gay families is the reaction of others:

When children are younger though they can be a bit confused and don't understand that someone can have two mums or two dads because their family isn't like that. This means they sometimes have lots of questions for children who have gay parents. Sometimes other children can be mean about gay people because they have never met any gay people and don't know much about them. Some people make judgements about what it's like to have gay parents. They think children will have a certain type of life and not as good an upbringing. Children with gay parents can find these judgements upsetting. Children with gay parents like having gay parents and wouldn't want things to change but wish other people were more accepting.

(Guasp, 2010, p. 3)

Recent research shows that 98 per cent of young gay people hear 'that's so gay' in school and we know from polling evidence that teachers don't necessarily respond to it when they hear it. Children with gay parents told us that it affects them too.

(Guasp, 2010, p. 17)

Parents with English as an additional language

When children who do not speak English join a setting, there is, inevitably, an advantage if there are practitioners who do speak their language and, therefore, who can help to understand and reassure a child during the transition. Key people will be working intensively with the child, valuing the home language but also introducing new vocabulary in order for the new language to develop and evolve. Parents, too, who do not speak English, may feel lost as they navigate within a system which is not familiar, in a language which also is not familiar. If these language barriers are not resolved, parents may not only feel more isolated within the setting but may also experience further inequalities through difficulties accessing further support, such as health care: 'Those within minority ethnic communities are often the most disadvantaged and also in greater need of health, education, social welfare services but are often least able to access these services readily due to communication difficulties' (Children England, n.d., p. 3).

Within the Equality Act 2010 (Government Equalities Office, 2010), there is a requirement not to discriminate on the grounds of race and, by supporting families whose language is not English, it is possible for settings to give parents a positive and supporting experience which could impact their progress in gaining support beyond the setting.

This support can be:

- translation services (either formal or informal) – there are some barriers to this also, including costs, the interpreter's own knowledge and understanding of the issue, misunderstanding and confidentiality (Children England, n.d.)

- ensuring that all families feel included and are able to participate in their children's care and learning experiences in the setting (DfES, 2007, p. 8)
- ensuring effective two-way communication of information via interpreters, written translation or the internet (DfES, 2007, p. 9)
- reflecting on your provision for children and families for whom English is an additional language, challenging your own knowledge, skills and understanding (DfES, 2007, p. 9).

Children with disabilities

Whether it is a family member or a child attending your setting, the family as a whole will feel the impact of a disability in terms of income, family dynamics and parenting time (as opposed to caring time) (Beresford *et al.*, 2007).

Parents who have a child with a disability can feel that they have lost 'aspects of their personal identity' (Beresford *et al.*, 2007, p. 2) as the needs of the child may have an intensive effect on the family and how their life can be run. Raising a child with a disability might be expected to be stressful but, in one paper, parents claimed that:

> it is not caring for the child which causes the stress but the processes which the families have to go through to access provision or to have the children recognised by professionals as more than just a sum of his or her 'deficits'.
>
> (Hodge and Runswick-Cole, 2008, p. 640)

Those parents who had positive experiences valued the professionals' sense of collaboration, open-mindedness, responsiveness and 'a willingness to take on new perspectives' (Hodge and Runswick-Cole, 2008, p. 645).

Strengths-based practice

Strengths-based practice has evolved in response to the deficit model of working with families, which removed power from service users and applied an 'expert model' (Davis *et al.*, 2002), with a resulting power base positioned within the professional sphere. So parents were perceived as the problem, which experts would 'fix'. The principles behind strengths-based practice are more positive, with an aspirational ethos which recognises that most families want what is best for their children, know their children very well and have a considerable amount of expertise to offer in terms of planning and support for children. Even when parents do not seem to care, or whose children display behavioural problems, strengths-based practice avoids judgement and blame as it recognises that environmental factors influence lives (Scerra, 2011) and looks for positives through a belief in the possibilities for change and the power of hope. The approach recognises that the hope and trust that practitioners place in parents promotes resilience to work through challenges rather than crumble underneath them.

Pattoni (2012, p. 2) summarises the key points of strengths-based practice:

> Strengths-based approaches value the capacity, skills, knowledge, connections and potential in individuals and communities.
>
> Focusing on strengths does not mean ignoring challenges, or spinning struggles into strengths.

Practitioners working in this way have to work in collaboration – helping people to do things for themselves. In this way, people can become co-producers of support, not passive consumers of support.

Strengths-based practice has a focus on the partnership model of working with people, which also emphasises relationships and trust-building. But it is not without its challenges or critics. First, Pattoni (2012) points out that evidence to support the practice is only just emerging. It can also challenge the practitioners who may be moving from the expert, or possibly the befriending model, to the partnership model (see page 79 of this chapter), which is facilitative and collaborative in its delivery. Pattoni says:

> The experience of working in a strengths-based way may be difficult for practitioners, particularly because they may need to re-examine the way they work to being more focused on the future than on the past, to focus on strengths instead of weaknesses and from thinking about problems to considering solutions.
>
> (Pattoni, 2012, p. 13)

Take a look at these activities relating to strengths-based practice (CWDC, 2010). They will help to illustrate the point that it is important to look beyond the surface issues and look at fundamentals.

Activity

Read the case study* below, then consider the Higgins family from a deficit position. Discuss with colleagues. Next, look at it from a strengths-based position. How are the Higgins family doing? Does it make any difference to focus on strengths in order to see the positive aspects in place for these children?

The Higgins family seem to have a lively and somewhat chaotic lifestyle. They have seven children, ranging from three to 14 years of age, together with three large dogs. Their small house is always full of lots of friends and family. Things are clean but very messy.

Rob Higgins travels a lot because he is a lorry driver. When you visit, he is often cooking or shouting at the children to sit down, clear up or shut up.

Lizzie Higgins and the family go to church almost every Sunday and it is here that Lizzie says she gains her strength for life. The two older children are in the choir.

Rob brings his children back presents from his travels and the family often go out for dinner or get a takeaway the night he returns. He is home about one week in four.

The children spend a lot of their time at a park about a quarter of a mile away. Many of the Higgins children are athletic and play football, the girls included.

Some of the older children have had occasional problems at school, such as not completing their homework or getting into verbal and even physical fights about someone 'dissing' a sibling.

The eldest child was recently caught smoking cannabis at the park.

The Higgins children are popular amongst their friends and, other than the odd skirmish over possessions, they seem to get along with one another.

What have you found out from this thumbnail sketch? You may think that this family is verging on the dysfunctional, with drug use, shouting, fighting, messy home and children and animals all over the place. But if you look closer, you will find many elements that increase resilience in their lives.

For example:

- There are two adults involved in raising this family, so they benefit from support, additional income and a partner to share responsibilities with, all of which reduce risk factors (Stewart *et al.*, 1997).
- Whilst untidy and chaotic, it is possible to see employment, application of boundaries and a strong and united family where siblings look out for each other.
- Liz goes to church, two of the children are in the choir; also a couple of the children engage in sport. Involvement in outside activities is another strength to increase resilience (Siraj-Blatchford *et al.*, 2011).

See if you can find any more examples of resilience in this family. Before moving on to the next case study, consider how easy it is to make assumptions about people on the basis of what is going on on the surface. Then think about Tracey and what her story might be concealing (CWDC, 2010).

Activity

Now look at Tracey. Read Case A and discuss in groups before moving on to Case B. Discuss what you have learned from it.

Case A*

Tracey is a single, female head of household in a vulnerable low-income family. She has a two-year-old daughter, is seven months' pregnant and, for the last four months, has been caring for her 13-year-old niece. They are living in cramped accommodation.

Tracey has stated she wants to stay at home with her newborn baby for at least six months and has refused assistance to go on a training programme.

Tracey and her occasional live-in boyfriend, Kyle, are both 21 years old. Kyle is unemployed and on jobseeker's allowance. Kyle is in and out of the family home apparently not living there.

What would you be thinking or feeling about Tracey?

(CWDC, 2010)

Case B*

Kyle and Tracey live with their two-year-old daughter and Tracey's 13-year-old niece. They are expecting another baby in two months. Both adults are 21 years old and they have been together for four years. The flat is ordered, clean and well kept.

When Tracey requested a pre-school placement for her daughter, she said, 'She's so bright and I want her to have lots of opportunities to learn and meet other children'. Tracey also requested after-school care for her niece and the possibility of her having a mentor or someone to talk to as she is worried about her. Tracey's sister died in a road accident six months ago.

Tracey says six months after her baby is born, she'd like a job training herself so she can contribute to the family finances to make sure the kids get the best.

Kyle recently lost his job due to the recession and his company closing down. He has written 32 job applications and thinks he may have found a part-time job to supplement his benefits. He wants to do everything he can to support his family. Kyle has moved back to his mum's at present to give space for Tracey's niece to settle in and to sleep with her aunt as she is having nightmares.

What would you be thinking or feeling about Tracey?

Consider again the conclusions you have drawn from thinking about these two case studies. It is clear that one message is not to judge a book by its cover, but what else have you learned? Perhaps the importance of support in order to develop resilience? As a practitioner, families can gain from your support, building self-esteem, supporting and listening.

The partnership model of working with parents

Davis *et al.* (2002) wrote about the partnership model of working with parents in their textbook *Working in Partnership with Parents*. This model (Table 6.1) was used for the training courses run by CWDC for outreach workers, *Families Going Forward* (CWDC, 2010). This illustrates the different approaches and it is possible to see clearly the possible outcomes of relationships based on these definitions.

Activity

Discuss the pros and cons of working within these models. Consider when you might use a combination of them. Discuss how you avoid crossing boundaries.

As will be seen from the quotations in my research (see page 69 of this chapter), the message that friendliness has a strong influence on the atmosphere of a setting is clear. The practitioners were more likely to temper this with 'respect' and 'professionalism', but there is a distinction between friendliness and 'befriending', which should not be overlooked. By looking at Table 6.1, it can be seen where the boundaries lie. Befriending can sometimes cause boundary problems and can also be seen to exclude parents with whom you are not so friendly. So friendliness, warmth, knowledge and interest are positive and productive, but be wary of treating any parent who you find easier to get along with differently to another.

'What do you think makes a setting parent friendly?' – findings from my research

There are, of course, the obvious aspects of inclusive practice that reflect the community which is within that environment. A review of the setting's provision, perhaps using an environment audit such as the Early Childhood Environment Rating Scale (Harms *et al.*, 1998), followed by discussions with members of staff, will help to develop ideas and reflect on existing strengths and areas for development. My research, which was undertaken with parents and practitioners, showed that there was a strong overlap between their views on what made a setting parent friendly, and the responses indicate that in fact the importance of friendliness, warmth, smiling faces and a welcoming and open-door approach were common factors to both groups. Practitioners tended to

Table 6.1 A comparison of the partnership, expert and befriending models of working with parents

The partnership model	The expert model	The befriending model
• Parents and helpers actively work together – involved and actively participating. • Parents and helpers both influence decisions on what occurs. • Parents and helpers value each others' knowledge, strengths and expertise and use these in complementary ways. • Parents and helpers reach agreement on what they are trying to achieve and how. • Parents and helpers resolve disagreement or conflict through careful negotiation, beginning from the parent's position. • Parents and helpers show mutual respect and trust, involving interest, care and awareness of each other. • Parents and helpers communicate clearly in ways that show openness and honesty.	• The helper is assumed to be the expert with superior knowledge. • The helper leads and controls the interaction. • The helper structures the interaction regarding time, venue, content, etc. • The helper formulates the nature of a parent's problem by providing a 'diagnosis' and defining the outcomes for the parent. • The helper elicits information to support their formulation of the parent's problem or needs. • The helper is driven by their personal and/or agency's agenda in formulating outcomes for the parent. • The helper is not explicit about their role, their agency's agenda or how they came about their deliberations. • The parent is assumed to be relatively deficient in knowledge. • The parent is assumed to need the expertise of the helper. • The parent is assumed to accept and be compliant with what is offered.	• The helper engages with parents in a warm and friendly manner. • The helper may be perceived as offering an invitation to friendship. • No clear expectations of the relationship. • No clear boundaries of the relationship. • The relationship may feel circular. • The parent may think that the helper has no expertise. • No clear model or frame for working through a problem. • No start and finish. • Parents may feel less alone and isolated. • Parents may be enabled to have increased social skills. • The parent may sort through problems without expert intervention.

Source: Children's Workforce Development Council (CWDC, 2010).*

associate this with the skills related to these approaches, such as 'eye contact', 'polite' 'approachable' and 'open attitude'. They used words relating to friendliness, but they also linked these with 'professionalism' and 'respectfulness'. This may illustrate the challenge between developing friendliness with parents whilst keeping a respectful distance and relates to the partnership model of working (see above).

Parents also used specific examples of how this friendliness might present itself, such as 'friendly faces', 'kindness' and 'remembering names'. It was also important to them that practitioners showed a 'genuine interest'. For both parents and practitioners, the importance of time to spend 'getting to know families' was a high priority. Practitioners noted the importance of talking and listening and of being available to parents to 'offer support when requested' and to 'listen to the needs of parents as well as children'. Importantly, the listening was accompanied by a note of caution: 'don't judge', 'listening to suggestions', 'open attitude' and, as one practitioner said, 'From the first visit explain they are the most important and knowledgeable people in the child's life – we need their help to learn about the child'.

For both groups, whilst it was important to have clean, suitable spaces for meetings, and notices with information on them, far more important was friendliness, approachability and time. Also, it was not only the actions of the setting to work in partnership but the approach:

- 'Recognising parents' expertise in their own children and lives, doing things with families rather than to them is crucial.'
- 'Asking parents what they would like to run.'
- 'Providing information on raising children.'

Summary

All the evidence on ways to work closely with parents and to make a setting parent friendly links overwhelmingly to the relationship with the parent. Many nurseries and pre-school settings do not have the space to provide a separate room to ensure privacy so there are often challenges in establishing a strong relationship from the outset, especially for those families where you feel that more support is important.

Relationships with parents will benefit from the use of strengths-based practice as this supports opportunities for change and optimism. It is linked to the work of Carl Rogers relating to unconditional positive regard (Rogers, 1957). Not only can relationships benefit from your own behaviour but also the documentation that the setting produces. In order to reinforce messages to parents about their value, make documents and notices as inclusive as possible – it is not about who you include, but wording materials broadly enough so you do not unintentionally exclude anyone. Use generic terms – 'partners' rather than husbands/wives – but be specific in letters when you know names, and do not assume that the mother is the first port of call when a child is ill.

Finally, reflect upon how equal your relationship is with parents and whether the direction of information is one-directional or two-directional. Check how much input parents have for meeting times. Consider where parents can feel an ownership within the relationship. The elusive feature of time can enable practitioners to reflect upon and modify practice. The benefits of *making time* for this type of activity, possibly as a team, can be judged through the outcomes, and can be a valuable product for the investment.

Next steps...

A parent-friendly environment is one that supports a range of family members, encouraging their involvement and participation in the life of the setting.

The following links will take you to articles about fathers' involvement in settings. They could be used as the focus for a discussion on ways to encourage further involvement with fathers in your setting: www.earlychildhoodnews.com/earlychildhood/article_view.aspx?ArticleID=400; www.fatherhoodinstitute.org/2005/outcomes-of-father-involvement/.

Notes

* These materials are from the training resources *Families Going Forward*© CWDC, DfE and Juliet Neill-Hall. They have been used, with thanks, and permissions from Juliet Neill-Hall and subject to the availability conferred on these materials on the National Archive website under the Open Government Licence v3.0.

References

Asmussen, K. and Weizel, K. (2009) *Engaging and Working with Fathers*. London: National Academy for Parenting Practitioners.

Beresford, B., Rabiee, P. and Sloper, P. (2007) *Outcomes for Parents with Disabled Children, Research Works*, 2007–03. York: Social Policy Research Unit, University of York. Online: www.york.ac.uk/inst/spru/pubs/rworks/aug2007-03.pdf (accessed 19 December 2014).

Blanden, J. (2006) *'Bucking the Trend': What Enables Those Who Are Disadvantaged in Childhood to Succeed Later in Life?* A report of research carried out by the Department of Economics, University of Surrey and the Centre for Economic Performance, London School of Economics on behalf of the Department for Work and Pensions. Leeds: Department for Work and Pensions.

Burgess, A. (n.d.) *The Costs and Benefits of Active Fatherhood. Evidence and Insights to Inform the Development of Policy and Practice*. London: Fathers Direct.

Children England (n.d.) *Supporting Children and Young People Whose First Language Is Not English (Briefing)*. Online: www.childrenengland.org.uk/upload/Language%20Briefing.pdf (accessed 18 December 2014).

Children's Workforce Development Council (CWDC) (2010) *Families Going Forward Learner Resources* (written by Juliet Neil-Hall). Online: http://webarchive.nationalarchives.gov.uk/20120119192332/http://cwdcouncil.org.uk/families-going-forward-learner-resources (accessed 14 December 2014).

Davis, H., Day, C. and Bidmead, C. (2002) *Working in Partnership with Parents*. London: Pearson.

Department for Education and Skills (2007) *Primary National Strategy: Supporting Children Learning English as an Additional Language. Guidance for Practitioners in the Early Years Foundation Stage*. London: DfES. Online: www.naldic.org.uk/Resources/NALDIC/Teaching%20and%20Learning/ealeyfsguidance.pdf (accessed 18 December 2014).

Fatherhood Institute (2011) *Trends in Father Involvement in the UK*. Online: www.fatherhoodinstitute.org/2011/fi-research-summary-fathers-mothers-work-and-family/ (accessed 18 December 2014).

Field, F. (2010) *The Foundation Years: Preventing Poor Children Becoming Poor Adults: The Report of the Independent Review on Poverty and Life Chances*. London: HM Government.

Government Equalities Office (2010) *Equality Act 2010: What Do I Need To Know? Disability Quick Start Guide*. London: Government Equalities Office.

Guasp, A. (2010) *Different Families: The Experiences of Children with Lesbian and Gay Parents*. University of Cambridge: Stonewall for All. Online: www.stonewall.org.uk/what_we_do?2583.asp (accessed 16 August 2014).

Harms, T., Clifford, R.M. and Cryer, D. (1998) *Early Childhood Environment Rating Scale*. New York: Teachers College Press.

Hodge, N. and Runswick-Cole, K. (2008) Problematising parent–professional partnerships in education. *Disability & Society*, 23(6): 637–647.

Holmström, R. (2013) Gay and lesbian families and gay and lesbian parenting. In G. Knowles and R. Holmström (2013) *Understanding Family Diversity and Home–School Relations*. London: Routledge.

Nutbrown, C. and Clough, P. with Frances Atherton (2013) *Inclusion in the Early Years*, 2nd edition. London: Sage.

Pattoni, L. (2012) *Strengths-based Approaches for Working with Individuals. Insights: Evidence Summaries to Support Social Services in Scotland*. Glasgow: Institute for Research and Innovation in Social Services. Online: www.iriss.org.uk/sites/default/files/iriss-insight-16.pdf (accessed 4 August 2014).

Rogers, C. (1957) The necessary and sufficient conditions of therapeutic personality change. *Journal of Consulting Psychology*, 21(2): 95–103.

Scerra, N. (2011) Strengths-based practice: the evidence. *Discussion Paper. Uniting Care Children, Young People and Families*. Research Paper no 6 – July 2011. Parramatta, NSW: Uniting Care Children, Young People and Families.

Scourfield, N., Yi Cheung, S. and Macdonald, G. (2014) Working with fathers to improve children's well-being: results of a survey exploring service provision and intervention approach in the UK. *Children and Youth Services Review*, 43: 40–50.

Siraj-Blatchford, I. (2014) Diversity, inclusion and learning, in G. Pugh and B. Duffy (eds) *Contemporary Issues in the Early Years*, 6th edition. London: Sage.

Siraj-Blatchford, I., Mayo, A., Melhuish, E., Taggart, B., Sammons, P. and Sylva, K. (2011) *Performing Against the Odds: Developmental Trajectories of Children in the EPPSE 3–16 Study*. Department for Education Research Report DFE-RR128. London: DfE.

Stewart, M., Reid, G. and Mangham, C. (1997) Fostering children's resilience. *Journal of Pediatric Nursing*, 12(1): 21–31.

Whalley, M., Arnold, C. and Orr, R. (eds) (2013) *Working with Families in Children's Centres and Early Years Settings*. London: Hodder Education.

Chapter 7

Making connections between home and setting

In this chapter, we shall be looking at:

* parents and practitioners: staying in touch
* survey findings about the ways settings maintain links with parents
* Epstein's typology of family involvement
* ways of maintaining communication, learning journals and Te Whāriki
* principles of Reggio Emilia educational pedagogy.

This chapter links to the following Early Years Teachers' Standards:

* 8.3 Take a lead in establishing a culture of cooperative working between colleagues, parents and/or carers and other professionals.

In a Parental Opinion Survey published by the Department for Education, two thirds of parents said they would like more information and help from practitioners (Department for Education, 2010).

This chapter does not intend to list all of the many and varied ways in which parents and settings have links. Many valuable and effective strategies are used in settings and they maintain sound opportunities for contact with families. But you might find it useful to read this chapter with a reflective hat on. The purpose of it is to encourage thought about change, adaptation, doing the impossible, reaching out, making links, experimenting – building trusting relationships in whatever way works best.

It is known that children's learning can be extended when links are made between the home and the setting which encourage parental involvement (Desforges and Abouchaar, 2003; Melhuish et al., 2001).

Parental involvement is defined as including:

* good parenting in the home
* intellectual stimulation
* parent–child discussion
* good models of constructive social and educational values and high aspirations relating to personal fulfilment and good citizenship
* contact with schools to share information
* participation in school events
* participation in the work of the school
* participation in school governance.

(Desforges and Abouchaar, 2003, p. 4)

The challenges for parents and practitioners of staying in touch

The early years sector is a hard-working sector, and parents are hard-working too. For both groups, finding more time in an already overfull day is challenging, so rather than thinking along those lines, you might want to consider alternatives rather than additions; smart thinking strategies which save time. And of course, the benefits to be gained from building links with families will save time in terms of consensus, mutual understanding and children meeting outcomes, with each group being prepared to go that extra mile. It can be seen as an investment rather than a drain on time. The key challenge is to make this possible without putting additional pressure on parents and also to enable practitioners to do their jobs effectively.

We know that workers in the UK work for longer hours than most of their counterparts in the rest of Europe (BBC, 2011). This applies to fathers also, who 'now work the longest hours in Europe' (Muschamp et al., 2007, p. 4). There has also been an increase in two-parent households of the 'proportion of households with two full-time earners ... from 26% in 2001 to 29% in 2011' (Modern Fatherhood, n.d.). Given that the figures for part-time workers in the same survey has reduced, it would seem logical to assume that there are fewer part-timers because they have moved to full-time work. Whilst more people are working full time, it might have been hoped that the technological revolution would increase the time available to be with families, as workers make contact through Skype and email, reducing the need to spend additional time away from home commuting. But there is some feeling that:

> although at face value [technology] may seem to reduce stress by allowing families to work from home and increase the time that parents and children spend together, [it] may have actually increased the amount of time that parents spend working.
>
> (Knopf and Swick, 2008, p. 420)

So more people are working full time, and flexible working may be resulting in home time being taken up with phone calls from the office, emails picked up on smart phones and parents going back to their work once the children are in bed, leaving little time for rest and relaxation.

But we also know that it is beneficial for parents to be involved in their children's learning (Desforges and Abouchaar, 2003; Sylva et al., 2004). Perhaps one way to involve both fathers and mothers, whilst recognising the demands on parents' time, is to be 'more creative in our methods of establishing contact and involvement with families' (Knopf and Swick, 2008, p. 421), and to recognise the fact that 'fathers are much more likely than mothers to work full-time'. (Poole et al., 2013) and therefore it is more difficult for them to have as much time to engage in settings and family life.

Case study

One pre-school wanted to engage more parents in their setting. They were conscious that many parents could not leave work by 3.30 so they tended to see the same parent or childminder each time, rather than the wider family.

At a staff meeting, one of the practitioners suggested a 'family day', with a target that every parent who had a child at the setting would 'check in' at some point during the day, and tell the setting one thing that they liked to do as a family. The children would then build a family tree during the day and add parents' comments as they checked in. The parents could check in through Skype, email, the setting's Facebook or by coming in in person. They could even phone if they wanted! The end result would be a tree made by the children, and with pictures of their families on it, making a final, setting family.

The staff thought about what they would need to consider:

- How would parents check in?
- What about the parents who did not engage? How could they be encouraged and supported?
- How would parents be contacted so that they all knew about it?

Imagine this was a conversation going on in your setting. What could you do to take the idea forward? What would be the challenges and how could you overcome them? Would it work like this or would you need to modify it?

The author's survey findings about the ways settings maintain links with parents

The settings contacted in the author survey use a range of different activities to maintain links with parents. See Table 7.1.

The 'other' activities included some settings that offered parenting classes or courses, either about an aspect of child development, such as supporting your child in early maths, or more traditional parenting classes offering strategies on managing children's behaviour through the use of positive parenting skills.

Others mentioned the use of websites, webcams and access to online information.

Looking at Table 7.1, how does it compare with your setting? What does it tell you about the perceptions of parents and the perceptions of practitioners about the ways contact is maintained?

Table 7.1 Maintaining links with parents

Contact with settings	Parents (%)	Practitioners (%)
Newsletters	56	89
Texts	23	35
Emails	45	68
Children's activities supported across home and setting	27	59
Twitter	1.5	8
Facebook	11	9
Other social media platforms	0	6
Video links to settings	1.5	6
One-to-one meetings about child's development	41	64
Home visits	21	36
Informal conversations	47	43
Fundraising events	26	47
Invitations to setting activities	52	65
Invitations to participate at setting	27	57
Discussions on children's interests	36	45
Other	17	8

It seems that each example (except two) indicates a higher number of practitioners affirming that this is how they maintain links. The corresponding responses of parents are significantly lower.

For example, 45 per cent of parents compared to 68 per cent of practitioners state that the setting maintains links through email. How can the disparity be explained? Perhaps practitioners are emailing smaller numbers of parents, though this seems unlikely? Those whose children have been hurt in an accident during the day, or are poorly and need collection? This could mean that fewer parents receive emails on a regular basis, even though practitioners are emailing parents on a daily basis. It is also possible that parents do not have access to computers, which may explain the difference.

Another example is the 'invitation to participate at setting', where 57 per cent of practitioners assert that they stay in touch with parents in this way and yet only a quarter (27 per cent) receive those messages inviting them to participate. There are a number of possible explanations for this:

- Parents who have particular skills or job roles are asked (e.g. worker from public services such as a firefighter or a nurse).
- The same parents are asked on a regular basis; some parents are never asked.
- Parents who are not confident English speakers are not asked.
- Parents who are not already engaged in the setting are not asked because practitioners do not know enough about them to make the approach.

So it is possible that only a small group of parents, who are perhaps already known to the setting, are asked to talk to the children or work with the children. These are perfectly understandable reasons but the outcome remains the same – that some parents are not invited, ever.

The other point to note is whether the direction of travel of the information is one or two-directional. Does information flow in both directions or does it tend to move from one direction to another?

Activity
- Look at the list in Table 7.1 and make suggestions for the differences in the figures for parents and practitioners.
- Look at the list: what sort of information is being passed between parents and practitioners? How much information is being sent from the parent to the setting, or is the tendency that the information point is the setting and parents receive it?
- Look at the list: what does your setting do? How much information is two-directional? How do parents offer information about their children that you are able to use to shape policy, or to use in planning?

If we look again at Table 7.1, it is possible to see that only two strategies, the newsletter (56 per cent) and the invitations to setting activities (52 per cent), pass the halfway mark for these parents. Does this mean that another 48 per cent of parents do not get invited to setting activities, or that they do not perceive this to be a way of maintaining contact?

Informal discussions

Now we should look to the result that had the closest parity: informal conversations. There was considerable agreement between both parents and practitioners of this method of maintaining contact. It is also the best way of finding out more about families, using listening skills and open questioning to gather more useful information.

Activity

Informal conversations had a strong parity between parents and practitioners, but there are many challenges to their effectiveness. Discuss them in small groups, and consider how the challenges might be overcome.

Some research from New Zealand (Duncan *et al.*, 2006) looked at the ways in which parents were offered support. Parents fed back that they felt safe in the settings and found the care given to their children was reassuring.

However, it was the positive, trusting, known, stable relationships that were identified as the basis for building strong links between the parents and others in the early childhood (EC) centres and wider support agencies (Duncan *et al.*, 2006, p. 2).

The paper continues to explore the experiences of these families and also the 'strong philosophy that mainstream early childhood education have a strong role in supporting families' (Duncan *et al.*, 2006, p. 3). Clearly the parents are an important part of the children's network and through supporting them the well-being of the child is increased: 'Building stronger links between EC services, ante-natal programmes, parents and Whanau, parenting programmes, schools, and health and social services can also improve a child's educational achievements' (p. 4). The early childhood centres in New Zealand are similar to our own Children's Centres and would be located in areas of disadvantage, where more formal support opportunities such as parenting classes were available. However, there was a sense that attending parenting classes came a long way down the list of priorities when families were either overloaded with work or carried other stresses, such as paying bills and buying food. There was no time to learn to be a good parent.

But 'taking a genuine interest in the lives of family members was a strategy that was identified as helping families feel welcome, and supported' (Duncan *et al.*, 2006, p. 7). The key to the positive feedback from parents seemed to be the informal nature of the discourse, which put 'less pressure' (p. 8) on them.

So rather than being taught to be 'good parents' in a more formal situation, these individuals preferred the light-touch approach, whereby they shared information within trusted relationships with parents and practitioners, indicating a level of equality and two-directional information sharing rather than a more didactic and deficit-based approach.

If we return to the author survey findings, we could interpret this in the same way: that there is regular feedback and contact in informal moments between staff and parents, which would include dropping off and collecting children, but would also be more feasible in settings such as Children's Centres, whose purpose and structure would be similar to those explored in the research, and where there would be more space for parent meetings and informal chat. The value of the conversation is not just to share knowledge but also to increase the resilience of parents so that the supportive relation-ships with practitioners give them more strength to manage their situations (Duncan *et al.*, 2006).

Activity

If informal contact is a strength of settings, reflect upon the opportunities you have for doing so. Can you recall having conversations with parents that might have clarified an issue in their mind, or helped them to share concerns that were weighing on them that day? What skills did you use to support the parent?

Second, consider ways that this informal type of contact, which is spontaneous and generated from parental comments, could be replicated remotely? Can this be done through a social media forum, so parents have the opportunity to share questions if they cannot get to the setting? Might this be useful for those fathers who have less contact with the setting and might value a solutions-based networking opportunity with other fathers?

Development of trust as the prerequisite to effective communication

Throughout the literature, the message comes loud and clear: unless there is a trusting relationship, all forms of communication will be less effective and meaningful, and the early investment in getting to know families as individuals helps to avoid a tendency towards 'one size fits all'. As Knopf and Swick note:

> In order to increase the ability and tendency of early childhood professionals to establish meaningful relationships with families and ultimately increase active family involvement and collaboration between schools and communities, early childhood professionals must possess an understanding of the goals, cultural values, experiences and social supports that parents bring to school.
>
> (2008, p. 421)

They argue that the development of trust is 'absolutely essential' (p. 421) and it involves a 'paradigm shift' (p. 421) about the importance of knowing parents in order to support education.

It is important to remember that you, as practitioners, have long hours and a chal-lenging job too. The benefits of engaging with parents can, though, make the job of the early years practitioner more satisfying, enriching and effective. Through looking at the different ways that parents may engage with settings, it is possible to start identifying work that is already in place and consider planning beyond that.

Epstein's classic typology of family involvement

It is impossible to discuss parental involvement and ways that this takes place without reference to Joyce Epstein's work in this field (Epstein, 1995). Although Epstein's main work took place in schools rather than early years settings, there are enough parallels to draw upon that it maintains its relevance to early years.

Epstein's philosophy was that, like Bronfenbrenner's model of ecological systems (1979), there were a range of institutions within which children 'learn and grow' (Epstein, 1995, p. 702): schools, families and communities. These institutions are spheres of influences which can either be 'drawn together or pushed apart' (p. 702). When the spheres of influence overlap, there is communication and connections between the groups and the child at the centre is more likely to receive consistent and consensual messages from all spheres. Epstein uses the term 'partnership' through-out her work, and demonstrates ways in which this partnership can work together to make the schools more family-like, the families more school-like and so on. In this way, the knowledge, needs and experiences of parents are as much a part of the equa-tion as the needs of the school to educate and the community to participate. The two-directional nature of the engagements are an important way to capture know-ledge equally and empower all spheres. She suggests six possible types of communica-tion, ranging from parenting information from setting to parent, to empowerment within decision-making opportunities and wide collaboration. The six types of involvement are shown in Table 7.2.

As can be seen in type 2, communicating, Epstein stresses the importance of school-to-home and home-to-school communication. She notes that: 'Underlying all six types of involvement are two defining synonyms of caring: trusting and respecting' (Epstein, 1995, p. 711). So looking at Epstein's chart, you can probably see examples in your own practice that fit within each type. Think in particular about the two-directional aspect of communication, and consider how much information and dialogue comes from the family.

Activity

Looking at the types of family involvement in Table 7.2, consider whether you think these methods are appropriate for pre-school children. Is there anything else you would add, or alter?

Table 7.2 Epstein's six types of family involvement

Parenting	Helping all families establish home environments to support children
Communicating	Designing effective forms of school-to-home and home-to-school communications
Volunteering	Recruiting and organising help and support from parents
Learning at home	Providing information and ideas to families about how to help students at home with curriculum-related activities
Decision-making	Including parents through in-school decisions, developing parent leaders and representatives
Collaborating with the community	Integrating resources from community (businesses/other schools/civic awareness)

Source: An adaptation of Epstein's typology of parental involvement (Epstein, 1995, p. 704).

Other ways of maintaining communication

Focus groups or nurture groups

Rebecca Kirkbride (2014) has looked into the involvement of parents in nurture groups in a primary school. Although the children were older, it is still possible to see the relevance to early years in the ways that Kirkbride interviewed both staff and parents and noted the importance of communication, which 'needs to be clear and two-directional, while adopting an approach that is non-judgemental and empowering' (Kirkbride, 2014). You may have a small group of families whose children have particular needs, perhaps social and emotional, whose parents would value the opportunity to meet together for support and information. Perhaps vulnerable families if you are working in a Children's Centre. Margy Whalley uses the nurture group as one way to support vulnerable families at the Pen Green Children's Centre (Whalley et al., 2013).

Whilst the nurture group offers important opportunities to support children who have particular needs, there are challenges too:

- Some settings have little additional space for the groups to meet.
- Parents may be more reluctant to engage in the process if they feel labelled by the needs of their children.
- The group leaders would need to be experienced and attuned to the needs of parents, as 'parental role construction, feelings of agency and a sense of efficacy need to be developed in order for parents to be involved in their child's school experiences' (Kirkbride, 2014, p. 98).
- The support of a multi-agency team might improve the outcomes of the group, and this may be harder to muster in daycare or pre-schools than in Children's Centres.

This option calls for experienced and trained staff who are able to support the needs of parents as well as the needs of children, but the beneficial elements are considerable for higher need families, whether that is through social or economic disadvantage or disability.

Learning stories/learning journals

Parents, both mothers and fathers, have one key priority in common with the setting – the child. A warm and genuine shared interest in a child's development and learning can be used to build relationships, and certain resources can be used to enhance dialogue. For example, many settings use a version of Margaret Carr's learning stories (Carr, 2011) not only to engage the child in their own learning through discussion and sharing ideas, with use of photography and video capture, sharing ideas for new learning, but also to initiate a two-directional dialogue whereby practitioners learn more about the child and the child's experiences through listening to family stories and histories with children and their parents. More often called learning journals in the UK, these portfolios are rooted in the philosophy of the New Zealand early years pedagogy called Te Whāriki, which, according to Margy Whalley, is an 'approach which focused on the child within the family context' (cited in Lee et al., 2013, p. 1).

The Te Whāriki curriculum is founded on the following aspirations statement: 'To grow up as competent and confident learners and communicators, healthy in mind, body and spirit, secure in the sense of belonging and in the knowledge that they make a valued contribution to society' (Lee *et al.*, 2013, p. 23). Of the four main principles, two of them relate to relationships.

In many ways, the EYFS (DfE, 2014) reflects these principles through the theme of 'Positive Relationships'.

Learning journals are a valuable tool to use with parents, as they can be taken home by families to read and enhance, so that all participants actively contribute to the learning of the child, who is empowered by having a role in their own learning. There is now an electronic version of the learning journal that can be accessed online. Through the transfer and sharing of the contents, practitioners can learn more and ask children questions about the contents of the journal when it includes photographs from home – so the child becomes more familiar and is likely to want to share more information about home and family life.

Not all settings use the learning journal but many do, and those that do not tend to have similar structures in place. The effective use of this type of documentation feeds the relationship and in turn supports the child's sense of self and developing identity. This could be categorised under Epstein's typology (1995) as number six: collaborating.

Activity

Are you using learning journals? Can parents take them home with them? How do you ensure that they come back? Do you have agreements with parents? Does it matter if they don't bring them back?

The Reggio Emilia philosophy

The history of the educational and community-based pedagogical approach of Reggio Emilia had its origins at the end of World War Two, when funding was made available to the community in order to rebuild facilities that had been destroyed in the war. The sense of community in the region and the apparent aspiration to create positive experiences from the devastation of the war meant that the Reggio Emilia movement drew upon local support, resources, labour, optimism and hope for the next generation of children. As a result, the philosophy of the pre-schools in the region is deeply rooted in collaboration with the community, dialogue, discussion and collaboration.

The philosophy of Reggio is reflected in many aspects that we see in day-to-day practice in nurseries and Children's Centres. For example, in Reggio practice, 'parents have always been actively involved in the development and management of early childhood settings of Reggio Emilia' (Thornton and Brunton, 2005, p. 20). They are represented on the advisory council.

The importance of close relationships is paralleled in this philosophy too:

> Each class of children has two teachers who work together as a team. As the children progress through the infant-toddler centre or the preschool they stay with the same team of teachers, giving the opportunity for relationships between the staff, children and their families to be nurtured over a long period.
>
> (Thornton and Brunton, 2005, p. 26)

Time and space for staff to meet together, to meet with parents, to plan, to document, to prepare resources and to study are recognised as vital in supporting the teacher in his/her role.

(Thornton and Brunton, 2005, p. 26)

Activity

Consider your own practice in your setting and compare with the quotations above. What are the challenges of working in this way? What are the benefits? Have you made changes which reflect this philosophy? Do you think different types of setting would find this more or less challenging? What are your reasons for thinking this?

Summary

There is a range of ways to stay in contact and maintain engagement with families, but there is no 'one size fits all' approach. The two-directional nature of engagement ensures that the voice of the parent is heard as well as the institution, thus empowering parents and giving them some agency within the setting. Methods of engagement might not just include visits to the setting but remote opportunities through social media and internet. Informal contact can have as much value as more formal contact meetings, but it will depend on the type of setting that you are in as to what you can work with. The mindset that this is creating more work and therefore more pressure on you as practitioners might be challenged by the theory that, through this investment, you are reaching more parents and therefore better able to work effectively with children.

Next steps...

Parental pressures and time poverty result in the need to find alternative methods of communication in order that parents have a chance to see their children's learning and development. For a growing number of settings, one solution is the use of online tools and resources, including online learning journeys or cameras in the nursery. The importance of vigilance and safety precautions when using these tools is clear, and organisations such as NSPCC have developed a range of courses to maintain and encourage good practice when transmitting materials online: www.nspcc.org.uk/what-you-can-do/get-expert-training/keeping-children-safe-online-course/.

References

BBC (2011) UK employees work longer than most EU neighbours. *BBC News Business*. Online: www.bbc.co.uk/news/business-16082186 (accessed 5 August 2014).

Bronfenbrenner, U. (1979) *The Ecology of Human Development: Experiments by Nature and Design.* Cambridge, MA: Harvard University Press.

Carr, M. (2011) Young children reflecting on their learning: teachers' conversation strategies. *Early Years*, 31(3): 257–270.

Department for Education (DfE) (2010) *Parental Opinion Survey 2010. DfE-RR061.* London: DfE.

Department for Education (DfE) (2014) Statutory Framework for the Early Years Foundation Stage. London: DfE.

Desforges, C. and Abouchaar, A. (2003) *The Impact of Parental Involvement, Parental Support and Family Education on Pupil Achievements and Adjustment: A Literature Review*, RR433. Nottingham: DfES.

Duncan, J., Bowden, C. and Smith, A.B. (2006) A gossip or a good yack? Reconceptualizing parent support in New Zealand early childhood centre based programmes. *International Journal of Early Years Education*, 14(1): 1–13.

Epstein, J. (1995) School/family/community partnerships: caring for the children we share. *The Phi Delta Kappa*, 76(9): 701–712.

Kirkbride, R. (2014) 'They were a little family': an exploratory study of parental involvement in nurture groups – from a practitioner and parent perspective. *British Journal of Special Education*, 41(1): 82–104.

Knopf. H.T. and Swick, K.J. (2008) Using our understanding of families to strengthen family involvement. *Early Childhood Education Journal*, 35: 419–427.

Lee, W., Carr, M., Soutar, B. and Mitchell, L. (2013) *Understanding the Te Whāriki Approach: Early Years Education in Practice*. Abingdon: Oxon.

Melhuish, E., Sylva, K., Sammons, P., Siraj-Blatchford, I. and Taggart, B. (2001) *Social Behavioural and Cognitive Development at 3–4 Years in Relation to Family Background. The Effective Provision of Pre-school Education, EPPE project* (Technical Paper 7), DfEE. London: Institute of Education.

Modern Fatherhood (n.d.) *Key Facts and Figures*. Online: www.modernfatherhood.org/themes/fathers-and-work/?view=key-facts-and-figures (accessed 6 August 2014).

Muschamp, Y., Wikeley, F., Ridge, T. and Balarin, M. (2007) *Parenting, Caring and Educating. Primary Review Research Study 7/1*. Interim Report. Cambridge: University of Cambridge. Online: http://core.kmi.open.ac.uk/download/pdf/309511.pdf (accessed 15 December 2014).

Poole, E., Speight, S., O'Brien, M., Connolly, S. and Aldrich, M. (2013) *Fathers' Involvement with Children*. Briefing Paper funded by Economic and Social Research Council. Online: www.modernfatherhood.org/publications/fathers-and-families/ (accessed 6 August 2014).

Sylva, K., Melhuish, E., Sammons, P., Siraj-Blatchford, I. and Taggart, B. (2004) *The Effective Provision of Pre-school Education (EPPE) Project Final Report. A Longitudinal Evaluation (1997–2004)*. London: DfES.

Thornton, L. and Brunton, P. (2005) *Understanding the Reggio Approach*. London: David Fulton.

Whalley, M., Arnold, C. and Orr, R. (eds) (2013) *Working with Families in Children's Centres and Early Years Settings*. London: Hodder Education.

Chapter 8

Identifying, reflecting on and reducing barriers to partnership work

In this chapter, we shall be looking at:

*   barriers perceived by parents
*   barriers perceived by practitioners
*   theories of social and cultural capital in relation to parental involvement in early years settings.

This chapter links to the following EYT Standards:

*   1.3 Demonstrate and model the positive values, attitudes and behaviours expected of children.
*   2.7 Understand the important influence of parents and/or carers, working in partnership with them to support the child's well-being, learning and development.
*   5.1 Have a secure understanding of how a range of factors can inhibit learning and development and how best to address these.
*   8.1 Promote equality of opportunity and anti-discriminatory practice.
*   8.3 Take a lead in establishing a culture of cooperative working between colleagues, parents and/or carers and other professionals.

Returning to the history of partnership with parents

As we saw earlier in the book, one of the original purposes of parental involvement within schools and nurseries was to encourage them to find out more about the 'right' way to bring up their children, as the role of education was to compensate for the shortfalls of parents in society (Muschamp et al., 2007). This is likely to have coloured the nature of relationships with parents and had an impact on parents' understanding of their own role within education. This deficit model has slowly been eroded, partly through policy changes which are based on a better understanding (through research literature) of the knowledge and skills that parents have and pass on to their children. The philosophy now is more egalitarian and equal, with a clear recognition that parents have important information about their children and that practitioners should listen to them carefully as sharing knowledge will lead to greater gains and attainment for children.

But the legacy of the deficit model of parenting, and the presumption of superior knowledge of some educational practitioners, had led to some outstanding inequalities, even though policy has consistently moved towards a more partnership-based approach in recent years. As Muschamp and colleagues noted:

This emphasis on home–school partnership had begun to redress the problems of the deficit model of the previous decades but it did not remove the conflicting roles for schools. On the one hand teachers were to seek out partnership with parents in the education of their children, and on the other hand the detailed guidance and information that they were to provide for parents suggested that they were to continue to compensate for parental lack of ability or interest in education.

> (Muschamp et al., 2007, p. 5)

Tizard and Hughes (2002) also recognised and challenged the presumption that working class homes did not offer rich educational experiences. They produced a critique challenging the assumption that working class parents gave their children less rich experiences in terms of opportunities for talking and thinking (Tizard and Hughes, 2002). Their investigation proved that the quality and richness of the conversations were superior to some of those that the children experienced in school, as the teachers tended to assume that their capacity was not as wide. This is, argue Tizard and Hughes, because:

> It is nowadays widely assumed, almost without question, that professionals have a good deal to teach parents about how to educate and bring up children. The idea that professionals might learn from observing children talking to their parents at home has hardly been considered.
>
> (Tizard and Hughes, 2002, preface)

There are still barriers that act as limitations to effective and equal partnerships with parents, although these barriers do not exist in all settings, all of the time. But some of them probably exist in all settings some of the time. Some of the barriers are tangible, such as poverty stopping parents from being able to reach the nursery, or language barriers blocking effective and sensitive communication. Then there are other barriers that are less tangible, such as shortages of time to speak, listen and be heard, or the effect of social and cultural capital on people's sense of belonging and being heard.

In my research, some interesting findings emerged about factors that challenge partnership (see Table 8.1).

Table 8.1 Factors that challenge partnership with parents

Factors that challenge partnership with parents	Parents (%)	Practitioners (%)
Parents not engaging in the process	56	86
Practitioners not engaging in the process	35	53
Parents feeling unsure of their role	42	54
Practitioners behaving as 'experts'	36	55
Personality clashes between the key person and the parent	44	56
Disagreements about the child's needs	36	60
Not enough opportunities/activities in place to build relationships	38	45
Not enough time to build relationships	42	55
Not enough listening taking place	32	45
Other	15	9

This table shows that practitioners are consistently more aware of the barriers than parents. The wording of the question prompts a hypothetical response for factors that challenge the relationship so it is not obvious how much or how often these barriers are actually present, but it is clear to see that these options are strongly supported by both parents and practitioners.

There is much to reflect upon in this table, and the message that there are a number of barriers is clear, as is the self-awareness of the practitioners to some of the challenges of working with families. In particular, the response of 86 per cent of practitioners to the first option – parents not engaging in the process – which links to discussion further on in this chapter about power balances, deficit parent models and the lack of two-directional dialogue. The question on the lips of readers may be: why do parents not engage in the process ... what are the barriers? What can be done to turn this situation around so parents feel motivated and positive about their engagement with the setting?

There was also a clear sense from practitioners participating in the research that there was not enough time:

> I believe there is too much pressure on carers to do all different things and in the end we don't have enough time to speak to parents, which should be the most important thing.
>
> (Practitioner)

> Not enough opportunities to build relationships as in my setting we are limited to five minutes a day during feedback time, which I feel inappropriate and it reflects in my relationship with parents.
>
> (Practitioner)

Also, they were aware of the disadvantages of: 'Viewing the idea of partnership with parents holistically rather than on a case by case basis; every adult as well as every child is different' (Practitioner). For parents, the messages overall seemed to present the insecurities that could be experienced when engaging with the setting:

> Language problems – some parents might feel ashamed when they need help.
>
> (Parent)

> Lack of knowledge (parents don't know about the help they can get/where to get help).
>
> (Parent)

> When teachers fail to convince you that they actually think of your child as an individual, with individual, specific needs/likes.
>
> (Parent)

Activity

This research is a small-scale survey of practitioners and parents from a range of settings. Replicate the survey in your group, then discuss the findings. What similarities can you see, or differences? What conclusions can you draw from the findings? What actions might you consider?

Whilst, for many, the parent–setting partnership proves to be fruitful and positive so that all involved are focused on the individual child's well-being and development, there are a number of relationships where this is not so apparent. The next section will consider some of the barriers that have been identified through research literature.

Barriers to parental involvement

> Whilst there is a broadly held desire amongst parents for more involvement in schooling there are clearly material (time and money) and psychological barriers which operate differentially (and discriminatingly) across the social classes and individual differences amongst parents that operate within social classes.
>
> (Desforges and Abouchaar, 2003, p. 43)

In order to understand parental involvement, it is important to explore the barriers that are faced, and there is rich data to draw upon. Key to the understanding is that there are many ways to be involved with settings and schools, and parents might find some access points easier to manage than others. In one study (Kohl *et al.*, 2000), involvement with groups known to have risk factors (single parents, maternal depression and limited personal education) was measured across different forms of involvement (parent–teacher contact; the extent of parental involvement; the parent–teacher relationship; the teacher's perception of the parent; the extent of parental involvement at home; and the parent's endorsement of the school) and 'the different risk factors interacted differently with the various forms of involvement' (Desforges and Abouchaar, 2003, p. 44). So there are variations and subtleties and complexities within all findings.

For example, maternal depression was 'negatively related to every form of parental involvement except direct parent–teacher contact' (Desforges and Abouchaar, 2003, p. 44), whilst single-parent status was linked positively to involvement in the home, though negatively to the teacher's perception of the parent and the quality of their relationship. As is noted, the absence of the parent influences the impressions made upon practitioners, as: 'Not present in school, they run the risk of teachers' negative perceptions' (Desforges and Abouchaar, 2003, p. 44). It is easy to see how easily labels can be assigned to people in the absence of reflection on individual circumstances and the active refusal to pre-judge at all times.

Negative parental experience

There is evidence to suggest that a reluctance to become involved with settings and helping their children is related to parents' own childhood or adolescence: 'Parents' view of their role as teacher and their comfort level communicating with teachers and helping their children with school work may, in part, be a result of their own educational experience' (Kohl *et al.*, 2000, p. 2).

Activity

Saul has a two-year-old son. His own parents could not read or write and never visited the schools that he attended, because 'it's not our job to teach you, it's theirs'. The actual reason they kept a distance was because they felt embarrassed that they had literacy problems and remembered the way they were treated at school, as members of the traveller community. The experience had a long-lasting impact on them, leading to them to avoid the risk of humiliation when Saul was at school by keeping a distance. But this meant that Saul missed out because they did not come to parents' events and, before long, he stopped talking to them about his own learning (and the difficulties that he had) at school, having learned that it caused friction. Every time he did mention it, they told him that they had managed OK without GCSEs and he shouldn't worry about it. So he did stop worrying, and also stopped doing homework as nobody seemed to think it was important.

Now it is his son's turn to go to nursery. He is anxious that the situation will repeat itself but still hasn't broached this with his partner, Ann. The setting knows nothing about this worry, and they have recently notified Saul and Ann of the name of their key person and the dates for their son's settling-in sessions.

What sort of practice could help to support this family, without even knowing what the problem is?

   Think of ways that a setting can support parents like Saul in order to pre-empt any problems for him (and later on, his son).

Distrust of authority and safeguarding issues

Some families, who could be termed 'hard to reach', might be so because of previous brushes with organisations or other representations of authority. This could be because of the fear that they will then appear on the radar of an organisation which has links to social services and safeguarding officials. These barriers can be harder to break down because the parent is simply not engaged with the setting at all, but the outreach work that goes on through many Children's Centres and through the Family Nurse Partnership, which works intensively with teenage mothers during the first two years of a child's life (Brown *et al.*, 2012), supports those who find it hard to cross the threshold alone. In this way, parents have the opportunity to build a strong relationship with trained professionals whose role is to support and signpost to other organisations, such as Children's Centres or other childcare provision.

Forms of capital and the barriers they can create

Social capital refers to the social networks, norms and sanctions that facilitate cooperative action among individuals and communities.

(Halpern, 2005, p. 39)

Whilst social capital represents the influence of networks, social systems and communities within which we live and how these affect our lives and opportunities, cultural capital is about the impact that knowledge and understanding of a particular system, institution, language or expectation can make. Pierre Bourdieu (1986) argued that educational outcomes can be affected by a family's cultural capital. So rather than economic capital (i.e. money) being used to buy materials, or education, social capital is the benefit from contacts, networks and friends, and cultural capital is the benefit derived in a similar way but through background, education, skills and knowledge that would confer confidence and abilities and knowledge – and knowing 'the rules of the game' (Muschamp *et al.*, 2007, p. 4). French sociologist Pierre Bourdieu (1986) started from the hypothesis that:

> made it possible to explain the unequal scholastic achievement of children originating from the different social classes by relating academic success, i.e. the specific profits which children from the different classes and class fractions can obtain in the academic market, to the distribution of cultural capital between the classes and class fractions.

The converse of the advantages of being wealthy in social capital is that 'students from poorer families, having less capital, are seriously disadvantaged; attaining less well and having lower educational aspirations as a consequence, than students from more socially advantaged families' (Fuller, 2014, p. 131). If parents do not feel that they are likely to make a difference to their children's education, perhaps due to their own personal construct and internal working models (Fine and Fincham, 2013) and their own sense of self-worth, they are less likely to try, thus creating a self-fulfilling prophesy.

In her paper, Lareau (1987) demonstrated the impact of social and cultural capital through the investigation of the behaviour of parents from schools in different communities: one working class and one middle class. Whilst both sets of parents wanted the same outcomes for their children, the middle-class parents were more successful in supporting their children educationally because of their ability to derive information from their social networks in addition to the school, and their ability to support homework.

> Colton parents had virtually no social contact with other parents in the school, even when the families lived on the same street. The social networks of the middle-class parents provided them with additional sources of information about their child's school experience; the networks of working-class parents did not.
>
> (Lareau, 1987, p. 81)

Fuller notes that Bourdieu's hypothesis around the impact of capital has critics, but that 'as a theoretical tool for explaining differences in educational outcomes it has achieved some consensus' (Fuller, 2014, p. 132). In terms of what this means in practice, practitioners may wish to reflect upon whether they find some parents easier to get on with than others because they are similar to them. The expressions 'we were both speaking the same language' and 'we were on the same page' indicate an understanding, a clarity of meaning – sometimes understood non-verbally. This opportunity to share understanding may not be as available for a newcomer to the country, or someone who does not speak English well.

One-way traffic

Another potential barrier to open communication is a lack of opportunity for parents and families to have a voice because the flow of communication tends to move from setting to family.

Incentives which actively encourage families to become more involved in a child's setting are always welcome, and the Home–School Knowledge Exchange is one of these (General Teaching Council, 2008). The project looked at the different ways to learn more about children's lives outside school. They went about this by asking parents what they wanted from the school, and what they wanted to give the school, and how this information would be shared. Results were positive, although the researchers conceded that 'it is difficult to demonstrate direct impact ... as there are so many factors involved' (General Teaching Council, 2008, p. 3). They also noted: 'The researchers found that schools needed to be sensitive to feelings about power, exclusion, inferiority, language, ethical and privacy issues in the planning of home–school activities' (p. 3). And Muschamp *et al.* (2007) noted the importance of reflection upon how much of the exchange was one-directional.

However, one case study example showed the potential strength of this approach through its contact with a Gypsy Roma Traveller group, where disposable cameras were distributed to family, and children were asked to take photographs of their world. 'Much was learned' (General Teaching Council, 2008, p. 19), but it was also noted that:

> The Gypsy Roma Traveller children were much keener to discuss their photo-graphs while on the site and amongst their families than when they were in school, even in a small group of non-Traveller friends. This highlighted the difficulty in gathering data and information relating to Gypsy Roma Traveller children and the sensitivity which needs to be shown in planning such a project.
>
> (p. 19)

So we can perhaps learn from this project that the setting-based approach to planning activities related to learning about families and communities, in terms of initial engage-ment, preparation, sensitive communication, respect and interest, can facilitate gather-ing knowledge which, without necessarily removing barriers altogether, may help to identify clearly what the barriers are.

Activity

Listening to children and families

Discuss the ways in which you endeavour to maintain the voice of children and families through a two-way flow of information. Consider the prevailing direction of information and evaluate how much children and their families are heard and are represented in the setting. You may want to consider any other steps you can take and how you can develop practice in this area.

Working with members of the wider family, including fathers and separated fathers

Provision for the under-fives in the UK has a higher representation of women than men in its workforce (Office for National Statistics, 2013) – a visit to most settings will confirm this. Whilst this may, in theory, lead to challenges in terms of ensuring that men – as parents or practitioners – feel at home in a setting, this misgiving does not take good communication skills into account, regardless of gender. The position of males in early years care and education is one that is increasing only gradually, but fathers (together with other family members) are much more visible in settings at this moment, so it is for the current workforce to ensure that their needs as parents and fathers are met through the skills of the staff in settings. For example:

By offering activities aimed specifically at fathers, at times when fathers want to/can access them, settings can develop activities in a father-friendly environment enabling men to feel welcome in what is traditionally conceived of as a female space.

(Kahn, 2005, p. 37)

It is sometimes perceived that fathers are disengaged with their own children's care and education outside the home, but if fathers do not know that their involvement can have a significant impact on their child's development, and if they have work commitments which limit their involvement, it may not be easy for them to participate in this aspect of their child's life, whether desirable or not for them.

The two most significant factors impacting on increasing fathers involvement in early years settings that were identified by practitioners were fathers' reluctance to be involved (42 per cent) and fathers' work commitments (28 per cent).

(Kahn, 2005, p. 7)

Kahn demonstrates that a significant percentage of fathers fail to be involved because of their work, but also that over 40 per cent are reluctant to be involved. It is for settings to reflect upon the reasoning behind this reluctance and to consider ways to reduce it. As in many new situations, it can be hard to walk through a door when one is not sure that there will be a sense of belonging on the other side.

However, whilst the legacy of Bowlby (1953) left us with the notion that it was the over-riding responsibility of mothers to raise children and bond with them, economic and social change in the late twentieth century and onwards has meant that the work-force is populated more equally by men and women since 1971, with the rate for men going down from 92 per cent to 76 per cent and the rate for women going up from 53 per cent to 67 per cent (Office for National Statistics, 2013).

The increased sharing of domestic responsibilities can only be welcomed as research has pointed clearly to the impact of the role of fathers and recognised that they play a part in the development of their children as well as mothers. For example, in one report, Blanden (2006, p. 15) states: 'For boys, having a father with little or no interest in their education reduces the chances of bucking the trend [i.e. moving out of poverty] by 25 percentage points.'

In general, fathers' involvement in settings is growing, but they are still a minority group in many nurseries. Given that their presence and their relationship can have a positive impact on children, finding ways of encouraging men into settings, to share and to act as a conduit for the movement of information, can work effectively for chil-dren's well-being. However, if fathers live apart from their children, there may be a communications barrier in terms of shared documents and letters.

Activity

Consider the different ways that you communicate with members of families and what you learn from them about the children in your setting. What works best in your setting in terms of involving fathers, or grandparents? How do you ensure that, if a child's parents are separated, both parties are welcomed equally in the setting? Is there anything you might want to do differently?

Cultural differences in childrearing

Working with parents from diverse cultural heritage means having an understanding and empathy towards a range of habits and customs. A mismatch of cultural assumptions can cause barriers unless the practitioner is able to reflect on the personal constructs of the families within the setting and avoid making judgements.

Activity

A new family has arrived in the neighbourhood and has started attending the setting. The mother meets the key person and tells her that she subscribes to the view of the Continuum Concept (Liedloff, 1986), whereby she has kept in constant contact with her baby for the past year. The baby has been familiarised with her close family members, her parents have used a sling to carry her and she sleeps in their bed.

As a practitioner, what would your approach to working with this family be?

Opportunities

There are many barriers that can be easily overcome within settings, and some that may take longer to change. But the will for improvement and development is an important aspect of reflective practice and therefore, through thought, training, open-mindedness and supervision, there will be many opportunities to implement new practice that might include parents more and therefore improve children's outcomes.

At-home good parenting

In Desforges and Abouchaar's substantial report on parental involvement, it was found that, regardless of the barriers, parental involvement 'in the form of "at home good parenting" has a significant positive effect on children's adjustment and achievement' (2003, p. 4). So it is not always necessary to engage directly with the setting, but it is important for a positive ethos towards education and towards 'shaping the child's self-concept as a learner and through setting high aspirations' (2003, p. 5) in order to build a successful educational ethos along with the school.

Slow and consistent trust-building activities that value the parental contribution and seek to identify suitable methods of interaction are more likely to encourage a relationship to blossom.

Technology

Today's technology can offer many opportunities to share knowledge and information with parents, and also offers opportunities for free, instant translation services. Modern technology can offer routes of communication between settings and parents so that busy working parents can engage with settings at different times of day. Settings use social networking pages and Twitter to contact parents and keep them up to date; it can also be used for closed-circuit filming in the setting. However, there are many safeguarding issues in relation to the use of technology, and most settings now have a 'no mobile' policy as a result of practitioners being found guilty of using their mobile phones to film abuse within a network (Plymouth Safeguarding Children Board, 2010). However, many settings now use a range of social media and web-based resources to maintain contact and inform parents. The range of options includes:

- Facebook pages for the setting
- Twitter
- texting
- online learning journals.

Some of these resources result in provision of information in more convenient modes for parents but they can also provide a forum and additional opportunities for parents to make friendships and build a community. Since not all parents use technology, other traditional methods can ensure inclusion and sharing information in a range of ways.

Supporting parenting/reducing the stigma of parenting support

There is an opportunity to make a difference to families and to parenting that is sometimes overlooked. EYFS practitioners spend a large part of their day working with children and their families, some of whom need additional support in order to reduce parenting problems and the chances of their children developing or increasing behaviour conduct disorders. Whilst parents may have parenting worries and fathers may feel isolated and disempowered, the practitioners have the opportunity to refer worried or stressed parents to other professional services in order to access expert help.

However, not all the parents who might benefit from a parenting programme either know that they are available or access them.

> One child in five has behavioural problems that can affect their future life chances, while 5% of children have the most severe behavioural problems, known as conduct disorder. Prevalence rates are twice as high among boys as girls and are higher among children from disadvantaged backgrounds.
>
> (Khan, 2014, p. 3)

Summary

Seeking help can make parents feel as though they are a failure, embarrassed and defensive (Khan, 2014), but the referrer can give parents information about other agencies, and also give them the confidence to use parenting groups. Khan's research shows that the strength of the relationship can make a difference to the success of the referral, especially with people 'who listened to concerns, were gently persistent, used non-stigmatising language and capitalised on brief motivational moments' (Khan, 2014, p. 13).

Next steps...

Here are some ideas, case studies and activities that can be discussed in staff rooms in order to reflect upon different ways to overcome barriers: www.conwy.gov.uk/upload/public/attachments/480/Removing_barriers_from_parent_participationEnglish_2.pdf.

References

Blanden, J. (2006) *'Bucking the Trend': What Enables Those Who Are Disadvantaged in Childhood to Succeed Later in Life?* A report of research carried out by the Department of Economics, University of Surrey and the Centre for Economic Performance, London School of Economics on behalf of the Department for Work and Pensions. Leeds: Department for Work and Pensions.

Bourdieu, P. (1986) The forms of capital. In J. Richardson (ed.) *Handbook of Theory and Research for the Sociology of Education*. New York: Greenwood. Online: www.marxists.org/reference/subject/philosophy/works/fr/bourdieu-forms-capital.htm (accessed 14 December 2014).

Bowlby, J. (1953) *Childcare and the Growth of Love*. London: Penguin.

Brown, E., Khan, L. and Parsonage, M. (2012) *A Chance to Change: Delivering Effective Parenting Programmes to Transform Lives*. London: Centre for Mental Health. Online: www.centreformentalhealth.org.uk/pdfs/chance_to_change.pdf (accessed 14 December 2014).

Desforges, C. and Abouchaar, A. (2003) *The Impact of Parental Involvement, Parental Support and Family Education on Pupil Achievements and Adjustment: A Literature Review*, RR433. Nottingham: DfES.

Fine, M.A. and Fincham, F.D. (eds) (2013) *Handbook of Family Theories: A Content-based Approach*. East Sussex: Routledge.

Fuller, C. (2014) Social capital and the role of trust in aspirations for higher education. *Educational Review*, 66(2): 131–147.

General Teaching Council (2008) *Research for Teachers: Home–School Knowledge Exchange*. Online: www.tla.ac.uk/site/SiteAssets/RfT1/06RE044%20Home-school%20knowledge%20exchange.pdf (accessed 17 August 2014).

Halpern, D. (2005) *Social Capital*. Cambridge: Polity Press.

Kahn, T. (2005) *Fathers' Involvement in Early Years Settings: Findings from Research*. Pre-School Learning Alliance Report prepared for the Department for Education and Skills.

Khan, L. (2014) *Wanting the Best for My Children: Parents' Voices*. Report for Centre for Mental Health. London: Centre for Mental Health. Online: www.centreformentalhealth.org.uk/publications/wanting_the_best_for_my_children.aspx?ID=700 (accessed 28 July 2014).

Kohl, G.O., Langua, L.J. and McMahon, R.J. (2000) Parent involvement in school: conceptualizing multiple dimensions and their relations with family and demographic risk factors. *Journal of School Psychology*, 38(6): 501–523. Online: www.ncbi.nlm.nih.gov/pmc/articles/PMC2847291/pdf/nihms-148599.pdf (accessed 17 August 2014).

Lareau, A. (1987) Social class differences in family–school relationships: the importance of cultural capital. *Sociology of Education*, 60: 73–85.

Liedloff, J. (1986) *The Continuum Concept*. London: Penguin Books.

Muschamp, Y., Wikeley, F., Ridge, T. and Balarin, M. (2007) *Parenting, Caring and Educating. Primary Review Research Study 7/1*. Interim Report. Cambridge: University of Cambridge. Online: http://core.kmi.open.ac.uk/download/pdf/309511.pdf (accessed 18 December 2014).

Office for National Statistics (2013) *Full Report – Women in the Labour Market*. London: ONS. Online: www.ons.gov.uk/ons/dcp171776_328352.pdf (accessed 15 April 2015).

Plymouth Safeguarding Children Board (2010) *Serious Case Review. Overview Report, Executive Summary in Respect of Nursery Z*. Online: www.plymouth.gov.uk/serious_case_review_nursery_z.pdf (accessed 17 August 2014).

Tizard, B. and Hughes, M. (2002) *Young Children Learning*, 2nd edition. Oxford: Blackwell Publishing.

Chapter 9

Concluding points

Skills and strategies for working in partnership

In this chapter, you will find:

- some key points from the previous chapters with a summary of the key skills and attributes that practitioners need to work effectively with parents
- ways to review practice in the setting – the use of *appreciative inquiry* (Lewis *et al.*, 2011) will be explored as a strategy to support practitioners and implement change within a positive and reflective model
- voices from research
- next steps.

This chapter links to the following EYT Standards:

- 5.1 Have a secure understanding of how a range of factors can inhibit children's learning and development and how best to address these.
- 5.5 Know when a child is in need of additional support and how this can be accessed, working in partnership with parents and/or carers and other professionals.
- 7.2 Establish and sustain a safe environment and employ practices that promote children's health and safety.
- 8.3 Take a lead in establishing a culture of cooperative working between colleagues, parents and/or carers and other professionals.

Some key points from this book

- Improving children's outcomes
- The importance of trust
- Regular training
- The use of the term 'partnership with parents'

Improving children's outcomes

Whilst working in partnership with parents is something that happens day in, day out when working with children, the effectiveness of the relationship in order to improve children's outcomes is more difficult to capture. The targeted support that is available to parents – for example, through evidence-based parenting programmes – is shown to be effective in improving the quality of parenting (Parsonage *et al.*, 2014). There is evidence that parenting programmes:

- reduce 'child problem behaviour' (Parsonage *et al.*, 2014, p. 27)
- 'improve behaviour among the siblings of children with conduct disorder' (Parsonage *et al.*, 2014, p. 28)
- 'improve the mental health and well-being of the parents themselves as well as of their children' (Parsonage *et al.*, 2014, p. 28).

Currently, there is not universal access to parenting programmes in England and Wales, although research in the USA on the delivery of a whole-population parenting training programme showed evidence of impact (Prinz and Sanders, 2009). There is, however, a workforce of skilled practitioners who can and do support and model positive behaviour towards children and who can refer and signpost when parents need additional support. There is evidence that, for GPs, there is an under-awareness of both the significance of behaviour issues and the routes for supporting parents, according to a GP survey (Family Lives, 2012, cited in Parsonage *et al.*, 2014) and this lack of knowledge may inhibit parents from seeking further advice. However, practitioners who work with parents regularly and can build up strong and supportive relationships which do not blame parents for child behaviour problems, but work with them within a strengths-based model, may be able to support parents in seeking help and developing effective strategies.

In research conducted by the Centre for Mental Health (Brown *et al.*, 2012) about the implementation of evidence-based parenting programmes, the matter of referral routes was explored. It found that there were a number of referrers into the parenting programmes system and also towards the Family Nurse Partnership programme which is a 'voluntary, preventive programme for vulnerable young first time mothers. It offers intensive and structured home visiting, delivered by specially trained nurses, from early pregnancy until age two' (Department of Health, 2012, p. 5). Early years workers are included in the list of referrers. The report goes on to say that 'our findings suggest that some professions have vital opportunities to identify and support the right parents into these programmes. Successful referral is the first step in improving outcomes for the children with the poorest life chances' (Brown *et al.*, 2012, p. 40).

Activity

Undertake some research into parenting support in your local area. Find out what the local authority offers and how you can inform parents in your setting about the support which is available. Perhaps you can request a visit from one of the teams delivering programmes, who might be able to talk to practitioners and inform about the referral process.

Finally, the authors of the survey note that:

> Parents who wish to disclose concerns are generally drawn to certain favoured settings and professionals and these settings can be critical conduits for early identification and referral. Our findings also confirm the importance of effective partnership working and the whole-system commitment to parenting; this acts as the foundation for successful identification and referral of parents and children likely to benefit from evidence-based programmes.
>
> (Brown *et al.*, 2012, p. 41)

This vision is reflected in the cross-party manifesto document *The 1001 Critical Days* (Leadsom *et al.*, 2014), which calls for a number of changes, including these that affect the early years workforce:

> The health and early years workforce should receive high quality training in infant mental health and attachment as standard, in order for practitioners to understand parent–infant relationships and the services required when difficulties arise. Specialist training should include identifying the 5–7% most seriously ill and at-risk parents...

> Childminders, nurseries and childcare settings caring for under 2s must focus on the attachment needs of babies and infants, with Ofsted providing specific guidance on how this can be measured effectively...

> Health and early years professionals should encourage parents to read to their children as an effective and straightforward way of strengthening early attachment and language development.
>
> (Leadsom *et al.*, 2014, p. 9)

The message for early years practitioners seems to be that the sector as a whole is in a strong position to support children and families but there is always room for more training and opportunities to reflect on best practice.

Trust, training and partnership work

As we draw the key themes for this book together into the summary, space must be made to reflect upon the professional development of the practitioner who works with parents. There are many training courses, documents and resources which relate to working with parents, and also to communication skills, both of which are important to practitioners building strong relationships with parents.

Supervision is a requirement of the Early Years Foundation Stage practitioner and skilled supervision can be used for professional development in supporting parents and managing the complexities of this relationship.

The findings from the research I undertook showed a strong overlap of suggestions to the question: 'What would you suggest to improve partnership work?'

For parents, the suggestions included:

- 'keeping a friendly but professional approach'
- 'more health visitor involvement to provide expert help'
- 'more listening'
- 'opportunities for parents and school professionals to build relationships'
- 'trying to get ALL parents involved in some way'.

From practitioners, feedback was dominated by two consistent themes:

- 'listening and more communication'
- 'making time to listen to what the parent has to say without being judgemental and without making them feel that they have restricted time'.

On the basis of these findings, a whole-staff approach to finding effective ways to communicate within time boundaries, to sharing views and concerns with sensitivity and being approachable and friendly to all could benefit settings, practitioners and parents.

One practitioner felt that training was needed for all:

> Training for anybody who comes into contact with any new parent – to be kindly supportive – is going to help the parent. If you take a school setting: if school was not an easy place for you and you go back to that place, you'll have all sorts of feelings, so if everybody could help you to create a good enough experience, if everybody had training in supporting parents, if everybody supported you to creating a good experience...? Because for me that would go back to being non-judgemental and listening. But it starts really early and it is easy to get on the right or wrong track. So each meeting with a professional, from the receptionist upwards, whoever you come across, can validate and build up a sense of confidence in your abilities and support where needed. If you've got a fragile partnership only one harsh comment can potentially turn the relationship around for a long time, and it takes a long time to undo that. It is important to value the parents and children as a unit together. People are much better at valuing children but if you can value the whole thing, holistically, it can build and it can build trust.

This view of the importance of trust is reflected in Utting's review of research findings (2007, p. 1):

> Parents most in need of family support services are often the least likely to access them. Evidence suggests that engagement can be improved by: accessible venues and times for service delivery; *trusting relationships between staff and users*; a 'visible mix' of staff by age, gender and ethnicity; involving parents in decision-making; and overcoming prejudices concerning disabled parents, parents with learning difficulties and parents with poor mental health.

Professional development is an aspect of the Early Years Teachers' Standards (NCTL, 2013), and areas for training in settings might include:

*   building trusting relationships with parents
*   knowledge and understanding of local support provision and referral routes
*   sustained, shared thinking with parents
*   involving all parents: inclusive practice
*   compassion in practice.

Compassion in practice is closely linked to empathy, and strengths-based work is the discourse around 'compassion', which encourages the use of reflection and self-questioning on the part of the practitioner, such as: 'What values and beliefs am I carrying into relationships with children, parents and other teachers?' (Taggart, 2014).

Appreciative inquiry

One approach to whole-organisational work is appreciative inquiry (AI), which is a 'conversation-based change process' (Lewis *et al.*, 2011, p. 39). The model works through the use of five different themes: Define, Discovery, Dream, Design and Destiny, with 'action steps for each stage' (p. 39). The philosophy behind AI is to avoid any focus on problems but to identify opportunities to build and change an organisation, positioning itself within the successful elements of the organisation. In that sense, the principle of strengths-based practice has resonance within this approach. More information on appreciative inquiry can be found at: http://appreciativeinquiry.case.edu/intro/whatisai.cfm.

Moving forward with the 2014 EYFS and next steps

The Early Years Foundation Stage (EYFS) statutory framework has been streamlined and took effect from September 2014. The reformed EYFS takes forward some of the Government's changes recommended by the Tickell Review (Tickell, 2011). The reforms will aim to: reduce paperwork and bureaucracy; strengthen partnerships between parents and professionals; focus on the three prime areas of learning most essential for children's learning and development; simplify the age five assessment; and provide early intervention where needed, through the introduction of a progress check at age two. The Early Years Teachers' Standards (NCTL, 2013) also identify the range of work that professionals undertake within the early years, supporting parents, children and their colleagues. However, the challenge of time and economics continues to impede the pathway to widespread training. On the other hand, there is increased funding for pre-school places for two, three and four-year olds (HM Government,

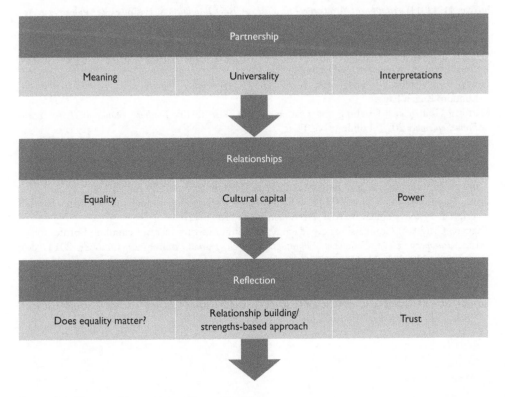

Figure 9.1 Partnership–relationships–reflection.

2014) which, together with an investment in positive training opportunities, which increase the knowledge and understanding of staff, may be influencing factors in improving the outlook for children. Building relationships with all parents is the key, and I leave you with Howe's insightful comment: 'If positive change is to happen, it is most likely to take place in the context of a warm, responsive relationship' (Howe, 2011, p. 226).

Activity

Use the partnership–relationships–reflection model as a framework for reflection of your understanding of concepts related to partnership with parents.

References

Brown, E.R., Khan, L. and Parsonage, M. (2012) *A Chance to Change: Delivering Effective Parenting Programmes to Change Lives*. London: Centre for Mental Health. Online: www.centreformentalhealth.org.uk/publications/chance_to_change.aspx (accessed 15 December 2014).

Department of Health (2012) *Family Nurse Partnership Programme: Information Leaflet*. Online: www.gov.uk/government/publications/family-nurse-partnership-programme-information-leaflet (accessed 15 December 2014).

HM Government (2014) *Free Early Education and Childcare*. Online: www.gov.uk/free-early-education (accessed 15 December 2014).

Howe, D. (2011) *Attachment Across the Lifecourse: A Brief Introduction*. Basingstoke: Palgrave Macmillan.

Leadsom, A., Field, F., Burstow, P. and Lucas, C. (2014) *The 1001 Critical Days: The Importance of the Conception to Age Two Period*. Online: www.andrealeadsom.com/downloads/1001 cdmanifesto.pdf (accessed 14 December 2014).

Lewis, S., Passmore, J. and Cantore, S. (2011) *Appreciative Inquiry for Change Management*. London: Kagan Page.

National College for Teaching and Leadership (NCTL) (2013) *Teachers' Standards (Early Years) From September 2013*. London: NCTL.

Parsonage, M., Khan, L. and Saunders, A. (2014) *Building a Better Future: The Lifetime Costs of Childhood Behavioural Problems and the Benefits of Early Intervention*. Report for Centre for Mental Health. London: Centre for Mental Health. Online: www.centreformentalhealth.org.uk/publications/building_a_better_future.aspx?ID=699 (accessed 28 July 2014).

Prinz, R. and Sanders, M. (2009) Population-based prevention of child maltreatment: the US Triple P System population trial. *Prevention Science*, 10: 1–12.

Taggart, G. (2014) Compassionate pedagogy: the ethics of care in early childhood professionalism. *European Early Childhood Education Research Journal*, online 29 October 2014. doi: 10.1080/1350293X.2014.970847.

Tickell, C. (2011) *The Early Years: Foundations for Life, Health and Learning*. London: Department for Education.

Utting, D. (2007) *Parenting and the Different Ways It Can Affect Children's Lives: Research Evidence*. York: Joseph Rowntree Foundation.

Appendix

Early Years Teachers' Standards (NCTL, 2013)© DfE

Contains public sector information licensed under the Open Government Licence v3.0.

Preamble

Early years teachers make the education and care of babies and children their first concern. They are accountable for achieving the highest possible standards in their professional practice and conduct. Early Years Teacher Status is awarded to graduates who are leading education and care and who have been judged to have met all of the standards in practice from birth to the end of the Early Years Foundation Stage (EYFS). Early years teachers act with integrity and honesty. They have strong early development knowledge, keep their knowledge and skills up to date and are self-critical. Early years teachers recognise that the Key Stage 1 and Key Stage 2 curricula follow the EYFS in a continuum. They forge positive professional relationships and work with parents and/ or carers in the best interests of babies and children.

An early years teacher must:

1 Set high expectations which inspire, motivate and challenge all children.

1.1 Establish and sustain a safe and stimulating environment where children feel confident and are able to learn and develop.

1.2 Set goals that stretch and challenge children of all backgrounds, abilities and dispositions.

1.3 Demonstrate and model the positive values, attitudes and behaviours expected of children.

2 Promote good progress and outcomes by children.

2.1 Be accountable for children's progress, attainment and outcomes.

2.2 Demonstrate knowledge and understanding of how babies and children learn and develop.

2.3 Know and understand attachment theories, their significance and how effectively to promote secure attachments.

2.4 Lead and model effective strategies to develop and extend children's learning and thinking, including sustained shared thinking.

2.5 Communicate effectively with children from birth to age five, listening and responding sensitively.

2.6 Develop children's confidence, social and communication skills through group learning.

2.7 Understand the important influence of parents and/or carers, working in partnership with them to support the child's well-being, learning and development.

3 Demonstrate good knowledge of early learning and EYFS.

3.1 Have a secure knowledge of early childhood development and how that leads to successful learning and development at school.

3.2 Demonstrate a clear understanding of how to widen children's experience and raise their expectations.

3.3 Demonstrate a critical understanding of the EYFS areas of learning and development and engage with the educational continuum of expectations, curricula and teaching of Key Stage 1 and 2.

3.4 Demonstrate a clear understanding of systematic synthetic phonics in the teaching of early reading.

3.5 Demonstrate a clear understanding of appropriate strategies in the teaching of early mathematics.

4 Plan education and care taking account of the needs of all children.

4.1 Observe and assess children's development and learning, using this to plan next steps.

4.2 Plan balanced and flexible activities and educational programmes that take into account the stage of development, circumstances and interests of children.

4.3 Promote a love of learning and stimulate children's intellectual curiosity in partnership with parents and/or carers.

4.4 Use a variety of teaching approaches to lead group activities appropriate to the age range and ability of children.

4.5 Reflect on the effectiveness of teaching activities and educational programmes to support the continuous improvement of provision.

5 Adapt education and care to respond to the strengths and needs of all children.

5.1 Have a secure understanding of how a range of factors can inhibit children's learning and development and how best to address these.

5.2 Demonstrate an awareness of the physical, emotional, social, intellectual development and communication needs of babies and children, and know how to adapt education and care to support children at different stages of development.

5.3 Demonstrate a clear understanding of the needs of all children, including those with special educational needs and disabilities, and be able to use and evaluate distinctive approaches to engage and support them.

5.4 Support children through a range of transitions.

5.5 Know when a child is in need of additional support and how this can be accessed, working in partnership with parents and/or carers and other professionals.

6 Make accurate and productive use of assessment.

6.1 Understand and lead assessment within the framework of the EYFS framework, including statutory assessment requirements.

6.2 Engage effectively with parents and/or carers and other professionals in the ongoing assessment and provision for each child.

6.3 Give regular feedback to children and parents and/or carers to help children progress towards their goals.

7 Safeguard and promote the welfare of children, and provide a safe learning environment.

7.1 Know and act upon the legal requirements and guidance on health and safety, safeguarding and promoting the welfare of the child.

7.2 Establish and sustain a safe environment and employ practices that promote children's health and safety.

7.3 Know and understand child protection policies and procedures, recognise when a child is in danger or at risk of abuse, and know how to act to protect them.

8 Fulfil wider professional responsibilities.

8.1 Promote equality of opportunity and anti-discriminatory practice.

8.2 Make a positive contribution to the wider life and ethos of the setting.

8.3 Take a lead in establishing a culture of cooperative working between colleagues, parents and/or carers and other professionals.

8.4 Model and implement effective education and care, and support and lead other practitioners, including early years educators.

8.5 Take responsibility for leading practice through appropriate professional development for self and colleagues.

8.6 Reflect on and evaluate the effectiveness of provision, and shape and support good practice.

8.7 Understand the importance of and contribute to multi-agency team working.

National College for Teaching and Learning (2013) *Teachers' Standards (Early Years) From September 2013.* London: NCTL. Online: www.gov.uk/government/uploads/system/uploads/attachment_data/file/211646/Early_Years_Teachers__Standards.pdf (accessed 14 December 2014).

Index

Page numbers in *italics* denote tables, those in **bold** denote figures.